D0777028

JAKUB TRPIŠ

THE
CHOICE

DEAR DEE DEE

WITH ALL MY HEART I WISH YOU TO BE HAPPY
AND HOPE THAT YOUR DREAMS COME TRUE

WITH LOVE, JAKUB
17.7. 019

2018

Imagine
the future.

Now imagine
the future is an illusion.

ISBN 978-80-907044-4-2

Prayer of the soul

Close your eyes. Stop perceiving the noise around,
And focus within.

Breathe in deep and slowly breathe out,
Like the ocean's ebb and flow.
Perceive the vast oceans within.

Breathe in deep and slowly breathe out,
Like the wind rustling in the leaves.
Perceive the great mountains within.

Breathe in deep and slowly breathe out,
Like the sun's aureola.
Perceive the endless universe.

Perceive the beauty here and now.
Savour this present moment.

Part one:

1/1 The car accident

t came like a bolt from the blue. Quickly donning his jacket, Tomáš could think of only one thing: If I'd guessed I'd be seeing Eliška for the last time this morning, I wouldn't have said good-bye that way at all. He hurried to the door and told the doorman what had happened.

'My wife has been in an accident! I have to get to the hospital.'

Though he was trying to get a grip on his feelings, tears welled up in his eyes. He couldn't find his staff card to open the door, but after an embarrassing silence that lasted some time the doorman let him through. Tomáš managed to thank the doorman, who called out after him sympathetically.

'It'll turn out all right, you'll see!'

Outside it was raining. He turned up the collar of his brown leather jacket to at least cover up his bare neck a little. The small, cold droplets fell quietly on the chill earth.

'Brrr, thank goodness I came to work in my car today. Otherwise I'd have to call a taxi,' he muttered as he rummaged for his keys in his pocket. He dropped them a couple of times before he managed to unlock the door. He couldn't recall how he got into the car, and he didn't regain his presence of mind until he'd been driving for several minutes.

That was a mistake. Better keep my eyes on the road now, he thought. He tried to focus all his attention on his driving, but various memories kept getting the better of him. He recalled the day they had got to know each other, and another thought took him back to the home where he had grown up. It was a cold day like today, and he introduced her to his parents. She kept checking to make sure she was doing the right thing – she was really nervous.

'Do you think they're going to like me?' she asked when they were on their own.

He just smiled and answered, 'Definitely not as much as I do.'

He was half-way to the hospital when he stopped at a crossing for a red light. The rain pitter-pattered on the metal roof – and from time to time the wipers creaked lazily across the windscreen. Trickles of water streaked seamlessly across the side window, each droplet going its own way, regardless of the others. Or were they complying with some precise preordained plan? His attention shifted from the droplets to the people crossing in front of him. Their expressions were vacant, as if their bodies were on autopilot, and their minds were somewhere else entirely. When he saw two lovers he paradoxically recalled the day he had confided to her that he wasn't sure if he still loved her. If he'd only known what pain he would cause, he would never have let those words pass his lips. It flashed through his mind that he had to tell her what he felt about her and how much she mattered to him. This thought was rapidly overshadowed by all the others. His body filled with an unusually strong urge to tell her everything. His heart beat twice as fast. He was startled by a car hooting behind him: the lights were on green and he was standing at the crossroads holding up the traffic.

When he had spoken to a hospital nurse on the phone she didn't tell him what had happened. He didn't know how seriously his wife had been injured, or if her life was in danger. The uncertainty was the worst he had ever felt in his life. He wanted to immediately be with her and feel she was safe. It took him some time to find his bearings in the hospital complex. At the emergency reception he told the nearest nurse his wife's name.

'I'll just ring my colleagues. Just take a seat for a moment please,' she quietly said, disappearing through a nearby door. The section was full of people, but nobody took any notice of the distraught Tomáš, who was so on edge that he couldn't even sit down. Is she all right? Or are the doctors fighting for her life at this very moment? Or perhaps…?! These thoughts kept going round in his head, as his mind taunted him with the darkest scenarios. Then it seemed to calm down and show him some far more optimistic possibilities. Perhaps they had just taken her to hospital for an examination, or maybe she just had concussion, he mused, letting his thoughts run their course. On the one hand he felt agitated and confused, while on the other he felt a sense of resignation. Eventually a senior nurse came up and asked him his name.

'Come with me, Mr Jedlička,' she said, heading towards a dimly lit corridor to the right. He followed her into a small, bright room that clearly served as a doctors' office. A thickset, gray-haired doctor was sitting at a computer. Next to the monitor there was a photograph of a woman holding a small boy in her arms (they looked very happy). When the doctor noticed how distraught he was, he immediately put him at his ease.

'Don't worry. Your wife is going to be fine.'

His eyes moistened and he felt an enormous sense of joy. Suddenly he felt several years younger.

The doctor continued, 'Your wife has had a severe shock, but fortunately there are no signs of any serious injury. Just to be certain we are going to perform some more tests on her to make sure she doesn't have any internal injuries. We're going to keep her in for another couple of days. You can see her if you want. She's in Ward C. Blanka here will tell you which room.'

Tomáš offered his hand and stammered, 'Thank you very much.'

The doctor just smiled and walked into a side room, where his colleagues were evidently going over a diagnosis.

Tomáš asked Nurse Blanka how to get to Ward C and headed off for it at a swift pace. On the way he could not help but notice the unhappy scenes that were taking place in one of the waiting rooms. A young doctor was telling relatives that their loved one had died. A fair-haired woman went into hysterics, while the man nearby tried to comfort her, without much success. At this moment Tomáš realized just how awfully fortunate he had been. Suddenly it was of no importance that there was a leak behind the chimney flue, that he had not received a bonus at work and that he had problems with his car. He walked through the door into Ward C and asked a nurse where he could find Eliška Jedličková.

'Room 7,' the tall young blonde answered, smiling at him as she continued to pass out medicine. He practically ran to get to Eliška as quickly as possible. So agitated was he that he did not even knock on the door. Before he managed to reach her she had sat up in bed. They embraced, and it felt like the most beautiful feeling in the world.

She burst out crying and blurted out, 'I didn't see it. That car. There were children inside.' And she began to sob again. He stroked her hair.

'It'll be all right, Eli. They'll be okay, you'll see.'

They kept hugging for a while without saying a word. After some time Eliška spoke.

'Karolína at work was supposed to come with me, but she was late and didn't answer my phone call, so I left on my own. When I eventually drove out, everything seemed okay.'

She then confusedly described the crossroads (while attempting to gesture, even though she could barely move her arms) where the collision happened. She should have given way, but she only spotted the other car at the last moment. At length she uttered:

'It hit me from the right. I don't know what would have happened if somebody had been sitting beside me.'

Tomáš listened to all this. It was extremely fortunate that Karolína had not gone with her that day. Then he told her everything he had been thinking about in the car.

'I don't know what I'd do if anything happened to you.'

'Just don't think about that, dear,' she answered, stroking his unshaven cheek. She loved the way he always put on a face when she did that. Then they carried on talking and talking. About important matters and silly things. They had not had such a good chat for a long time. Eventually a nurse appeared at the door with lunch, stating with a gruff expression:

'Your wife must get some rest. You should be on your way now.' She pointed at her watch. He kissed Eliška goodbye and disappeared through the doorway.

— • —

The next few days were of no great interest. It rained non-stop outside. Tomáš's family and friends often asked him about Eliška, who was released from hospital two days later. The passengers from the other car were also all right. Perhaps it was because of the accident that they both decided to take off for the mountains that weekend. They were able to spend three days at their best friend Ondra's chalet. Ondra always had a strange sense of humour. When he saw Tomáš's wife (with the scar healing on her forehead) he immediately started ribbing her:

'Why do you give us such worries, Eliška? Didn't you see the car or something?' and he started laughing. Tomáš now found this quite amusing.

On the Friday they headed off for the Jeseník Mountains. The chalet was quite high up with no road leading to it, so they parked the car in a parking lot below and they had to keep going on foot for another two hours.

Several rained-off days later the sky was cloudless, and it grew warmer. Having walked for about five minutes they met a young woman with an Alsatian dog running free without a muzzle.

'Don't be afraid, she's never bitten anyone,' her mistress smiled proudly.

'The fact she has never done it before doesn't mean I won't be the first,' Tomáš retorted, smiling to cover up his fear.

They walked deeper and deeper into the forest. Not a living soul to be seen. The further they got from civilization, the better Tomáš felt. The trees around them seemed to light up. He left the path a little when he saw a young fir tree some three metres tall. The ends of its branches had beautiful green needles. This year's growth, he thought, pulling one of the branches to his face. It had a magnificent smell, reminding him of his youth. He had spent a lot of time with his grandfather in the mountains.

He was naive in those days and thought he could change the world. He wanted to visit every single mountain, as well as places that were not even on the map. To be the first where no one had gone before. As he thought of his carefree childhood, he remembered the children he taught at school. He suddenly regretted the fact that he always removed their rose-tinted spectacles whenever they described what they wanted to be when they grew up. If I didn't do it then somebody else most certainly would, he had tried telling himself. Somebody has to tell them how the world works. He looked at the trees again, but now they just looked ordinary again. One more time he sniffed the young fir and set off at a rapid pace along the path after Eliška. By the time they arrived back at the chalet the sun had already set behind the ridge and the air had grown chilly. Everywhere peace and quiet. The orange glow on the horizon gradually faded into grey and a frosty autumn night settled over the mountains.

When they opened the creaking door they first checked to see how clean and tidy it all was.

'We mustn't leave it any untidier than we first found it,' she smiled.

'It's not that bad,' he decided, having gone over the chest of drawers opposite the fireplace with his finger, while flashing his usual little-boy smile. He lit a fire in the fireplace, while Eliška prepared a modest supper.

'Tomorrow we can go up to the lookout tower. What do you think?' he suggested.

'Do I have a choice?'

'Ah, you and your fear of heights,' he smiled slyly.

'Ah, you and your fear of dogs,' she retorted.

Tomáš rather enjoyed the evening. They reminisced about various incidents from the past.

'And do you remember what your father said when you brought me home?' she asked him.

'How could I forget? He yelled, "Thank God. I thought you were gay!" Then he fell on his knees and gave you a hug.' They both burst out laughing.

'It was only later that I understood your dad's really weird sense of humour.'

'Just like you have got used to mine,' and he stuck his finger up her nose.

'Hey,' Eliška laughed, as she defended herself. 'You are a dummy.'

But then she grew serious and her voice quivered. 'Whenever I close my eyes I see shards of glass flying everywhere, and my ears are shattered by the grating metal sound of those cars. I can't get the noise out of my head.'

He stroked her chestnut hair and embraced her, placing her head on his chest. The beating of his heart soothed her, and she soon felt safe. Her memory of the crash slowly dissolved, like ice thawing in spring sunshine.

Outside it was really cold and dark. The windows had misted up. The wood in the fireplace crackled as it gave off a pleasant warmth. The fire lit up the cosy room's walls with its hand-painted pictures of chalets and log cabins, which had hung there for over a century (each painting was dated). They chatted for a while and then made love. Over the last year their sexual life had not been all that passionate. They had tried to conceive. Recently his doctor had told him the worst: he couldn't have his own children. Perhaps that was why over the last few months their relationship had cooled. Perhaps that was why they didn't enjoy sex that much. They had tried so hard for a pregnancy that they'd forgotten what fun sex could be.

A thought passed throughTomáš's mind as he fell asleep: It wasn't that bad at all today.

1/2 Awakening

T omáš awoke to a chilly morning. It was still dark. The lights in the shelter did not turn on until seven o' clock, enabling him to at least tell if it was daytime or not. A strange smell wafted through the air, stinging his eyes. Like every morning he 'made himself' a glass of water, pouring it from a jerrycan into a little cup with an engaging faded kitsch picture of a dog on it, and tossed a chlorine tablet into it. It didn't go down very well, but he had become quite used to the peculiar taste, and it always made him think of the taste of clean drinking water. Of course, he was still a lot better off than on the surface, or even in an adaptation camp. Thousands of people that had been caught and successfully identified by the police and the army were taken off there every day. The civil war had been raging throughout Europe, and he had lost sight of who was fighting whom. He put his feet on the rough floor and shivered. It was cold and damp. He quickly put his shoes on and stood up.

He noticed his neighbour was not lying on his bed. It took him a while to realize he had perished in a roof-fall a couple of days earlier.

He walked out of a medium-sized dormitory, where some twenty of them were sleeping, and headed down a dark corridor towards the showers. The walls were dirty and wet. The hum of a giant ventilator pumping fresh air from the surface down to this part of the complex echoed along the empty corridor. It once used to be the underground Metro. During the war the underground tunnels had been used as shelters for hundreds of thousands of people. The fighting had rampaged all over the world. Dozens of atom bombs had fallen on China, the USA and Japan, while a new kind of virus, probably a biological weapon, raged across Africa. Europe had been ravaged by civil war, while Asia had seen a once-in-a-millennium famine and the continual waves of refugees could barely be contained in Australia, which as the only country that maintained neutral status was now struggling with huge overpopulation and pirate raids.

Nobody could now remember when the war had started. Nobody was sure which side this nation or that was on. Some countries changed sides during the conflict as often as their governments were replaced by various insurgent factions. People worldwide were plagued by fear and mistrust. Nobody could be sure if the next faction to seize power would find them inconvenient. The Czech Republic was now in a tug of war between movements made up of military personnel from Russia before its collapse.

People stopped saying what they thought and started parroting the opinions of those in power. Too many of their relatives had disappeared after they tried to change things. Tomáš's thoughts were suddenly interrupted by a scream. Perhaps someone has been robbed again, he thought. Eventually he got to the showers. The queue was shorter than usual, so it was soon his turn. Alas a five-minute shower a week barely patched up his ailing, languishing body, and he took care in the shower not to touch anything much with his bare skin, as various skin diseases were rife throughout the shelter. After showering, he went off to the canteen for breakfast. He bent over the dirty, greasy hatch and muttered between clenched teeth: 'Thirty-four.' Of all the meals served there, this one was at least edible, even if it bore about as much resemblance to ordinary food as chess did to other sports. As he ate he looked around. Everyone was staring at their own plate in silence.

Again he became absorbed in his thoughts. It might well have been awful in the shelter, but he was still very lucky. He was a healthy man with a decent background and an outstanding teacher. They had found him a job at the central shelter. Originally it was the Prague Metro, but that had stopped running soon after the first bombing raids had become a regular part of life. His job was now to teach the children of the leading politicians (that is, the ones currently in power) at a local school. He glanced at his scuffed old watch, gulped down a last mouthful and hurried off to his lessons.

The children in his class wore careworn, grown-up expressions. They should have been enjoying a carefree childhood, but they barely smiled and only spoke among themselves when it was really necessary. One little girl in a blue dress looked at him differently. When he looked her over he noticed bruises on her hand, while her face was greasy and almost expressionless. She looked like a doll that had been thrown into the gutter years ago. He often had to give her a shake to bring her round. Apart from teaching the children he also had the task of providing his biological material for selected women. Here his thoughts returned to Eliška. She should have been in the shelter with him, but something had gone wrong. The transport hadn't made it. Now she was almost certainly dead. He bowed his head and started to pound his forehead with his fist. Two children on the first row raised their heads for a moment, but then got back to their copying work.

Tomáš lost all hope when he found out about his wife's death. He would never forget that day. Everywhere was dark, dank and terribly cold. The frost and despair crept into the marrow of his bones, as if iced water were being pumped into his veins. There was nothing on earth to console him. He used the last of his money to buy adulterated alcohol and a rope, but at the last moment he was rescued. Nobody said anything to him. Suicides were frequent here. No one wanted to live like a rat underground. Nobody wanted a life without hope any more. The world had become a dark place. This darkness could be felt at every step and could be seen in the eyes of everybody he looked at. The little girl in the blue dress, who he had just been watching, stood up from her desk. Her pitiful, greasy face leant over his shoulder so she could whisper to him:

'The darkness is drawing in. The world will die, because you have stopped fighting for it. The world will be consumed in fire!'

'What darkness? What are you talking about?' he cried in horror. He woke up with these feelings and thoughts. It was all just a dream!

He tried to catch his breath, but with the same sense of despair as in the dream. He pressed his head to his knees, as tears ran down his cheeks. His heart thumped as if his life were in danger. He must have awoken Eliška too, as she began to stroke his sweat-soaked back: 'It was only a dream, dear. It's alright now.'

'Uh-oh. I thought those dreams were over.'

1/3 Problems

The weekend in the mountains was a pleasant interlude, but now he had to get back to the everyday routine of loan repayments, arguments with colleagues and giving his pupils a good talking to. Still, things were a little simpler now. On the Monday he was teaching until late in the afternoon. During the day his colleagues often asked him how Eliška was getting on after the accident. He always answered smilingly that everything was now just fine.

After lunch, which was not up to much, he could look forward to a civic studies lesson with 4A, his favourite class. One way or another they got round to a discussion on helping other people. One girl told a story about her cousin Jakub. He was twenty-five years old, in and out of work, expecting a child with his girlfriend and now they were deep in debt.

'Auntie and Uncle don't have much money themselves, and if anything their situation's getting worse. Who knows what they're going to do now?' she added.

'I'd leave them right in it,' Robert, the class smart-guy, smugly declared.

Lenka, the local hippy, snapped, 'You've always been clueless.'

Tomáš often gave his pupils some leeway for an exchange of views, which was another reason why most of the class naturally held him in great respect.

'What would you advise Jakub to do?' he asked, inviting them to engage in open discussion.

'Jakub's girlfriend should get an abortion,' said Lukáš, Robert's best friend.

Then Beáta floored him: 'You'll probably never get a bloody girlfriend,' and she added in a calm voice: 'I think they should go round all the banks and explain their situation. The banks would definitely agree to reduce the instalments.'

Dominik, Tomáš's favourite, joined in the discussion: 'Banks are only interested in profit. The women behind the counter will smile at you to persuade you that you need a loan, but when you go and tell them you can't pay it back they won't help you.'

'You're right, Dominik. You can't usually negotiate a reduction in payments, even though the banks' attitudes towards this have been changing in recent times. What would you recommend for Jakub?'

'The banks' attitudes are changing, because the banks realize it's better to get less money back from the clients than no money at all, so they're willing to come to an agreement. Jakub should ask his parents if he can move back in with them for a while. Then he could use the money he would otherwise have paid in rent to pay back his debts.'

Robert and Lukáš started laughing out loud at this, and Robert commented, 'Smartass, they'll be glad to get rid of a failure of a son like that.'

At this point the calm class debate turned into a pub brawl, as some five pupils started shouting at each other (while Lenka banged her textbook on the desk) and of course none of them could be heard. Tomáš looked sternly at Robert and Lukáš.

'Your parents must be really proud of you. Come out to the blackboard, both of you. I'll cut you down to size! The discussion's over, thanks to these two.'

The room resounded with a murmur of disapproval, more because the discussion was over than because the class smart-guys were being tested.

The test ended as expected. Robert got a bottom mark and Lukáš not much better, 'since you did at least try, Lukáš,' Tomáš explained.

The rest of the day's lessons were by no means ideal. He was supposed to go over the increasing incidence of bullying at school with the first formers, but they did not want to go along with this at all, and if anything actually defended bullying. Tomáš completely lost control of the discussion. The headmistress had warned him the previous time that if the situation did not improve between him and the class then another teacher would take over.

'Phew,' he came out of the class, exhausted. The corridor was empty and cold, with the same pictures hanging on the walls for years. Now he was feeling old and forlorn. Several pupils walked past and greeted him, but he only managed to grimace back. He then headed off to the staff room, where a weekly meeting was taking place. On the way he reconsidered Robert and Lukáš's test. Perhaps I was a little harsh on them, he thought.

The meeting was really seething. The school was having financial difficulties, and Honza was explaining why the grammar school was getting less money from the local authority than they had anticipated. Tomáš joined in the argument by responding to the idea that the local council could be given a fright by warning them that pupil numbers might be reduced: 'We can't just blackmail the council like that.'

'You've always been soft, sunshine. I can see you've never been in the army,' Karel challenged him, and Tomáš suddenly realized just how much he couldn't stand him. He only needed to bump into him in the corridor and his mood was immediately ruined. And now he was putting Tomáš down in front of his colleagues. Instantly he counterattacked: 'You're so henpecked you have to make up for it here at school!'

Karel was taking a deep breath to deliver the final death blow when he was stopped short by Jindřiška.

'Now, now, gentlemen,' she said with the calm and experience of many long years as headmistress. 'You won't resolve the issue that way. We have to be united. I suggest we meet up with the mayor to explain the situation to him. We can tell him that pupil numbers may be reduced, because that's the way it is. There's nothing else we can make savings on. Honza is well in there, so he can go over it all with him.

But he is definitely not going to blackmail anybody,' and with these words she looked sternly at Karel.

The meeting came to an end, so Karel came to wind up what he had started: 'We haven't finished yet, mummy's little pet.'

Tomáš wanted to respond somehow, but he couldn't manage any more than 'Sure'. The incident had robbed him of the last vestiges of his good mood.

On the way home he got wet. Apart from his damp socks he was beset by other problems that had been bothering him for some time. All afternoon and evening, in fact, he was weighed down with debilitating thoughts: debt repayments, hatred of Karel, his bad nutritional habits and other issues. What was more, he felt worse and worse physically.

He was irritable because he had to smile at everyone and act as if he were doing just fine. He was distraught, but couldn't tell anybody. Everybody wanted something from him, but he couldn't please everybody. He felt like a student at college. Every teacher thinks his subject is the most important, but these weren't teachers, these were his family, friends and colleagues.

He had the feeling that somewhere along the way he had lost an important part of himself, but he couldn't remember where and what it was. Then his thoughts started revolving around his nightmares. His throat dried up and he had to sit down. The very thought of them almost paralysed him. Eliška was not at home, so he felt all alone. The ticking of the wall clock was the most interesting thing in the apartment and indeed in his entire life. He went off to the local for a beer. When he came back home late in the evening she was already asleep. As he lay down beside her, he no longer had any doubts...

The feeling he had been fighting for so long, which had vanished after the car accident, had come back. He was lying beside his wife, and yet he felt so enormously remote from her. No matter how hard he tried, he could not get rid of the feeling. He felt like he was in his dream. Everywhere it was dark, dank and horribly cold. His bones and joints started to ache. A part of him had died. And then a little later it died again. This repeated death, return of hope and then death again was wearing him down. Depression engulfed his entire body. Thousands of thoughts raced through his mind. He couldn't remember when it happened. When he stopped loving her. The girl he wanted to spend the rest of his life with. That feeling of love following the car accident was only a side effect that covered up his problems for a while. Now he was forcing himself to love her like he used to. He didn't want to break her heart, as he had once long ago promised himself never to hurt her.

It had been going on all that year. He hadn't said anything to her. He had tried to once, but it didn't work out. Eliška guessed it when a month previously she'd asked him if he loved her. He hadn't been able to answer her properly then. She was fretting over him, but then she was pretending nothing was the matter just like he was. They were playing a game of happy couples, so that nobody around them ever found out it was all over. Eventually he had realized. He didn't want to hurt her, so they were acting out a performance of Look Everyone! The Happiest Couple in the World. Except the charade was actually hurting her far more.

The entire truth weighed down heavily upon him, pressing on his chest like an enormous boulder. He had betrayed her. He had betrayed himself. She would be a lot better off on her own than with a husband who didn't love her. Three months before that he was actually thinking of being unfaithful, and it was only his principles that had prevented him. He had finally understood that it was better to live alone than to live in a relationship that didn't work. But he didn't have the strength to change it.

Tomáš was now entirely engulfed by a feeling of total emptiness, self-betrayal, alienation and sadness. Financial problems at school, dreams of despair and his total torment regarding his wife meant that everything he thought of upset him. When he was twenty he'd always thought that by this time he'd have a well-paid job which he would enjoy. He imagined a wife he would love above all else, and marvellous children. Instead he was deep in debt with a tiny apartment and a relationship that was falling apart. He no longer enjoyed his work. And he had failed as a man since he hadn't managed to give his wife a child.

I'm thirty-two, I've achieved nothing in life and I hate myself, he concluded.

He felt like disappearing. He wanted to jump out of bed and get away somewhere. Anywhere. Just away from there. Away from that screwed-up life with nothing to grasp hold of and nothing to support him. It was over! The final performance. He no longer even had the strength to be annoyed.

I might just be better off if I don't wake up tomorrow, he thought as he fell asleep. It was dark, dank and horribly cold all around.

1/4 Difficult decision

When Tomáš woke up in the morning, it took him a long time to decide to open his eyes. He wasn't feeling any better. Fortunately the night had gone by without any more nightmares, or did he just not remember them? On the way to work he considered the situation again, with hundreds of thoughts gushing from his unquiet mind, until he was suddenly roused from his total lack of focus on his surroundings by a little girl.

'I can't find my little doggie. What am I going to do?' she sniffed. He couldn't guess where she'd come from. She wore red tracksuit trousers (muddy from the knees down) and a coarse yellow jacket. She held an empty leash, her nose was running, her freckled face was tear-stained and her ears were burning red – the perfect picture of misfortune.

Marvellous, my entire life up the spout, and now I have to go looking for some mutt, when I totally hate dogs! Whose idea was that, to send a little kid out to walk a dog? Probably something wrong with her parents, he silently vented, surprising himself at just how much anger he was holding in. He looked at the little girl smiling at him and did not even know why he offered to help her.

'He might have run off down to the river. Come on, let's go and have a look.' It was as if someone else were talking. They went down to the river in silence. The morning mist, which was now increasingly frequent, had thickened so much that visibility was down to a few paces. The little girl happily and noisily ran over to the nearby trees, where her carefree dog was taking itself for a walk. This cheered Tomáš up. Well, at least that's one problem sorted out, he thought as he hurried off to work. On the way he realized: I really must do something about that. I can't remember the last time I felt happy. I can't go on like this.

During the lunch break he had the idea of going off to visit the school psychologist, but then he immediately had second thoughts: I don't trust him that much. What if he told Karel? They're good mates. I really don't need any of that.

Suddenly he realized: Hold on! I could call my friend Klára. She had once mentioned someone she knew who helped her out of depression after a miscarriage. She said he was a marvellous guy, and ever since he'd helped her she looked far happier and more balanced, and she was determined to have another baby, which turned out to be perfectly healthy. He didn't want to say too much to her, so he preferred to sort it out using text messages. She gave him an exact address and arranged an appointment with Kohl for Thursday afternoon. That's what he was called. I'm feeling better already, he thought and the corners of his mouth lifted slightly.

Over the next few days he kept wondering if it made sense to go off to see some stranger and tell him his problems. Could it be a mistake? But then again this man had helped Klára come to terms with something as awful as a miscarriage. At length he told himself he would at least give it a try. He lied to Eliška that he would be held up at work and he headed off for the city centre, where Kohl had his office. It was a sunny autumn day. He ran up the stairs to a door marked Dr Martin Konečný, Psychologist and Healer, just as Klára had described. At the last moment he hesitated, but at length he knocked and went in.

He instantly caught the scent of marijuana. The battered cabinets were covered in odd pieces of paper, while the floor in the middle of the office was covered by a faded Persian carpet. Fresh, cold air wafted in through an open window, but otherwise the room was quite tidy, and everything there seemed to belong. In an old leather armchair a man was sitting, seemingly as old-fashioned as the rest of his office. He wore a loose, dark printed t-shirt, the kind that used to be worn years ago. His thinning curly hair fell down around his rather bronzed complexion. He must have been around fifty years of age. Going off Klára's description, he was the one.

Tomáš introduced himself.

'I am the light,' the man answered, taking another drag.

Tomáš stood there, stunned. He did not know what to answer, which clearly amused the man.

'My light greets you and the light that shines within you,' the man said with a smile, adding: 'Now come and park your backside.'

Eventually Tomáš managed to come out with a few words: 'And where am I to sit?'

Kohl took another drag, fixed his gaze on his guest for a while, making him rather nervous, and then retorted, 'There's enough room on the floor, but I'd recommend that Persian carpet. It's good to sit on, and we'll be able to see one other.'

Tomáš had expected all kinds of things, but not that! Feeling quite hard done by, he objected, 'What, am I to sit on the floor like some kind of menial of yours? I deal with people equal to equal, and I expect that from others.'

'You shall sit on the floor as my pupil. Your reaction surprises me. I thought you were further forward.'

He could not understand this at all. 'Your pupil? Further forward? You don't actually know anything about me!' he yelled, thinking some very unpleasant thoughts.

'I could smell your ego even as you were coming up the stairs,' Kohl struck back, yet all the while he had a singularly affectionate expression. And that was not all: 'You let yourself be governed by your ego – you are its prisoner. The ego is a good servant but a bad master. You're just thinking of your own problems. You have the feeling that the entire world has been plotting against you. You're unable to eat, sleep or make love properly. You commute to and from work like a zombie. That's not life, but slow death. You hate yourself for what you've become, but you're unable to admit it. You only look at yourself, and you don't notice the world around you. You have lost your spark. You've forgotten everything else completely. Everything! Do you still have the feeling that I know nothing at all about you?'

Again he was lost for words. He did not know how to react. The creaking of the armchair now just made him feel even more embarrassed. He decided to leave to escape the humiliation, but before he managed to say anything, Kohl smiled at him: 'You may go – our first lesson is over. Come back when you think it appropriate. My doors are open to you every Wednesday from two in the afternoon.'

'What? Come back here so you can put me down like that? Sure thing,' he retorted, silently adding: you moron, you! He did not even look at him, but just left without saying anything else.

As he stood in the doorway, Kohl called after him: 'You can be more than that!'

He thought he would explode with anger as he walked down the stairs. So distraught was he that he had no recollection how he actually got home. When Eliška tried to prize out of him what the matter was, he just fobbed her off.

'Oh, I've just got some problems at school.'

'Is it that Karel again?'

'I don't want to talk about it just now,' he snapped and went off to have a strum on his guitar. That was the only thing that could calm him down. His mind was focused on just one thought: I'm never going back there!

— • —

The next day he was unable to think of anything else. The man's a drug addict, who should never have been given medical accreditation, one part of him said. And what on earth did he have in mind when he called himself the light? Another part of him was asking. And what else have I entirely forgotten? Several voices were speaking together in his mind, but these two were uppermost. He was no longer so sure that he would not go back. The crank had something that he did not have. What was it? He wanted to know the answers to his life and he felt that Kohl could provide them.

Should he remain proud and never go back there or... seek for some meaning to life? As always, when he was unable to make a decision, he headed off for the mountains, where there was no one to bother him with constant worries, stupid comments and pretences. Today there was fog all around. The city was covered in smog and the sun looked like a full moon – barely visible. It looked just as cold and burnt-out as he felt. What was more, the city air smelled awful. Tomáš looked forward to getting away.

As soon as he got above the smog level, he was met by a marvellous view of an emerald cloudless sky. Up he went higher.

I'd almost forgotten how beautiful it is here, he thought. He took a drink from his bottle. He did not know anything that tasted as good as ordinary water, and he relished every sip.

He walked on even higher. The sunrays stroked his fatigued body.

He was even able to take off his jacket because it was far warmer here than in the smog-drowned city. Autumn was drawing to its end – these were the last warm days of the year.

When he got to the top he was almost a mile above sea level. He settled down in his favourite spot. There was a good view from here, and no hikers ever wandered by. What he saw looked more like an impressionistic painting than reality.

There wasn't a single cloud up above, although the river that flowed down into a valley to the south was lost in a sea of clouds below. The peaks that grew out of this ocean had as many colours as he could possibly imagine. The sun warmed his face pleasantly, and a gentle breeze blew. He did not know how long he was 'out of it', but he fell entirely under the spell of this artwork. He went back to his childhood. When he was eight years old he had once got lost in an unknown town. To this day, years later, the same horror would seize him. He wandered around streets that all looked alike, turning his head this way and that in search of his mum. Exhausted, he sat down on some grimy steps, buried his face in his little palms and whimpered. A short while later he heard her velvet voice: 'Here you are, my little angel.'

Little angel, he smiled.

Why am I so dissatisfied? Why can't I say goodbye to Eliška? Where have all those dreams gone? What actually happened at Kohl's? How come he knew so much about me? What is drawing me back there like that, damn it?! The feeling that he had to go back was all the stronger up there. When his mind had calmed down, only one thought remained: I must go back.

1/5 Soul and ego

Several days had passed since his trip to the mountains. Tomáš was beset by the same old apathy, slowly gnawing away at him and showing itself for the most part in his irritability. His colleagues and friends noticed that he was feeling down, but he always kicked their questions into touch. He knew he had to see Kohl on Wednesday, otherwise he would never dare go back. Now or never. On Wednesday he'd had normal afternoon lessons, but today they had been called off. So he could go. Now his dreams were repeating with almost daily regularity. Identical with just small variations. As if the needle had stuck.

He couldn't bear squeezing into public transport, preferring a brisk walk to Kohl's office in the centre. He ran up the stairs to the second floor. There was a slight whiff of marijuana in the air, but it was too weak to be recent. As soon as he walked through the door he was met by a similar sight to the one he had previously faced. The faded Persian carpet, the battered cabinets and Kohl sitting in an old leather armchair. As Tomáš entered the room he raised his head and smiled at him. Tomáš was surprised by something he had not previously noticed. Kohl's features were very distinctive. His eyes were wise and kindly, sparkling like those of a young boy.

'I'm very glad you've come,' Kohl began in a tender voice. 'I know it wasn't easy for you, but you have mastered the first lesson.'

Tomáš was taken aback. It was only after about thirty seconds that he let slip:

'What? What first lesson?'

Kohl closed his notebook and settled himself comfortably into his armchair, which gave out a long creak. He then started explaining:

'Above all, you have to regain control of your ego. It took you exactly twelve days. With time you will learn to handle it faster.'

'I was in quite some doubt, but in the end I decided to come. I really was very angry.'

'Doubts are quite normal, but you must not allow them to overwhelm you. Anger, feelings of guilt and fear are a gift. They tell you that you are dreaming a bad dream. They show you that you are living a false story. They warn you that you are living an irrelevant situation.'

Tomáš did not know why, but he poured everything out:

'Everybody has moved on, everybody has moved somewhere, but I have the feeling I'm going back. I feel lost. I have this feeling I'm in some kind of game, but I have no influence over its result. I don't have the remote control in my hand. As if I can only observe.'

'People often have it encoded somewhere inside them that life has to be a fight. Try putting your hands behind your head and waving them.'

Without thinking, he placed his hands behind his head and waved them, while asking: 'And is this going to he-elp?'

Kohl smiled broadly: 'No, but it gives me a good laugh.'

'You're just playing around with me again. Just like last time,' Tomáš retorted.

'Last time I did what had to be done to help you get out of your personal hell. Now I am trying to get you to learn to laugh at yourself.'

'What did you mean when you said I had mastered my ego?'

'That will be a long story. Now sit down on the carpet and listen carefully. Of course, you may ask if you do not understand anything,' and Kohl pointed down.

'Why do I have to sit on the floor like some menial?'

'I see you have no problem with honesty. That's good. You have to sit on the floor. That is the only way you are going to learn how to master your ego.'

He just grimaced and reluctantly sat on the floor beside Kohl, who began to explain:

'When you were born, your soul and your ego wished for the same thing – to breathe. This was the first and the most difficult task that we all face in life. Your entire being focused on this single objective. All your cells had to learn within a few seconds to live in a different world, in a world without your mother. The world of the womb was full of security, certainty and love. In the womb your soul and your ego were as one. Just as they were in the first months after you were born.'

Tomáš interrupted: 'And what does this have to do with my present difficulties in life?'

'Absolutely everything. Even months after your birth your soul and your ego were as one. You no longer felt as secure, because your mother sometimes went off, leaving you alone. Occasionally she would not feed you, when you were hungry, so you no longer felt that security. Sometimes something bad happened, you had a twinge of pain, so you no longer felt the safety of your mother's womb. One part of you automatically started to ask why. Soon afterwards the same part started to say that you had to somehow ensure that sense of security, safety and attention.'

'The ego – so that is when my ego was born!' Tomáš interrupted him again. This suddenly made him realize why his pupils would occasionally interrupt him.

'Exactly,' Kohl nodded. 'That is when your ego separated.'

'You're even worse than I am when it comes to hairsplitting. And that is saying something!' Tomáš grinned.

Kohl did not respond to this comment, but carried on with his explanation: 'The ego began to look for ways to make sure it had that feeling of security, safety and attention. It took command of your soul. The soul is able to obtain energy from itself. It is a kind of perpetuum mobile. The ego cannot do that, so it has to acquire its energy from the outside – from people. It tried all kinds of ways. Really, all kinds! At first it was still quite undeveloped, so it only knew one way –

crying. Whenever you didn't like something, you started bawling. Many people stay that way all the way into adulthood.'

'So the ego steals energy from other people. It cannot produce energy itself. Just like my sister. Whenever she doesn't like something, she bursts out crying and draws all the attention to herself. She really annoyed me that way when I was younger!'

'Yes, that is a very popular way. Even though it is very primitive, it works again and again on a lot of us. Some have attained a second level. If they don't like something, they start banging and smashing things until they get what they want. Unfortunately, their parents are too weak to stop them, so their children remain that way into adulthood. Aggression is a very popular way to acquire energy in today's patriarchal society. But then some children get even further. They keep asking their parents the same question until they hear a favourable answer. Some parents fall for that. Anybody who has stuck with this method of acquiring energy can be a very persistent debater in adulthood. They will pressure you into what they want to hear.'

'Yes, that is exactly how my father does it. And I know another aggressive type. Karel, a colleague at work. He harbours this tremendous resentment against me, I think. He would definitely very much like to smash my head against a wall, if it weren't socially frowned upon.'

'Oh yes, he's certainly done that a few times in his mind's eye.' Kohl smiled. Leaning back in his armchair, he looked out of the window for a while and continued:

'As a boy, Karel certainly tried other approaches – he tried to ask and he tried crying, but he succeeded most with aggression. Crying, asking and aggression – these are all ways to obtain energy. When you have enough energy you feel strong. That is the task of the ego. To construct the strongest stronghold, so that others cannot get at you, since the ego conceives all beings as separate. It considers each individual to be a danger to be protected against. This is a relic of our animal ancestors.'

'But there's nothing wrong with that. Everyone tries to protect themselves and their family.'

'But then I didn't say there's anything wrong with that, Tom, but it is bad, when this yearning for security makes you control yourself so much that it holds back your soul. Remember, when you were born, your soul and your ego were as one. They harmonized together. Then the ego separated, began to build its stronghold and unfortunately for you bricked in your soul. When you were little you were used to flying, having experiences, combining and then separating again from the souls of other people, but over time your ego built such a perfect stronghold for it that it gasps for breath. Not only have you bricked in your soul, but at the same time you have stopped taking other people's energy.'

Tomáš now felt he was being very much wronged. After all, he wasn't bricking his soul in! He wanted to explain this, but Kohl, who was clearly mistaken, did not let him get a word in edgeways:

'That is why, you've recently been feeling so out of sorts. That is why you're depressed and can't eat, sleep or make love properly. Your soul gives your life meaning. Without our souls we are just machines that get up in the morning, go to work, spend the afternoon emotionlessly performing meaningless activities and then just as vacantly, go home in the evening to sleep.'

Tomáš bowed his head and sighed:

'But then that's the way most people have it, and yet they're happy enough. They don't give their soul any space, they sap energy from others and live a relatively problem-free life. Why doesn't that work for me any more? I never asked anybody for this.'

'I know, I know. At first it is difficult. Nobody has any influence over when they start to wake up. It just happens all at once. At first it is all confusion, incomprehension and pain. But believe me, in time you'll be saying you'd rather live a soulful life full of problems than a soulless life. You can always sit in comfort and security at home, and you won't come to any harm, and yet when you close the door and lock it, all those bad things will not happen to you, but then neither will the good things either.'

Then Tomáš thought of his aunt. She often said something similar.

Outside the night was drawing in – the days were getting shorter. Kohl reached out to close the window, turned the handle and got back to his guest.

'Sometimes we basically do everything right, and yet we still feel unhappy, though of course it is at times when you feel the worst that you grow the most. You develop the most. I know you would like to sort it all out right now, get rid of that burden, but that is not what we are here for. We have to learn to live with that burden.'

Now Kohl was looking right into his glazed eyes:

'But don't worry. It doesn't happen to anybody until they are ready for it.'

At this, Tomáš's thoughts wandered to his dreams, but he did not yet feel enough trust in his new therapist to mention them. Instead he asked:

'So do I have to prioritize the desires of the soul over those of the ego?'

'Our task is to get into the childhood state where the desire of the soul balances out the desire of the ego. That is the only possible way to be happy. You cannot force your will on your soul. It doesn't work like that. Coercion is the tool of the ego. The soul does everything with love. Infinite love. It can take in so much energy that the ego has no more need for any more. That is how they get into equilibrium. The ego receives enough energy to feel strong, and the soul has its freedom and its new experiences.'

Kohl could see that Tomáš was still groping in the dark, so he brought up an example:

'Imagine a highly-placed politician who has achieved everything the ego could possibly desire. He has money, power and status, but he cannot allow himself to love anybody else, because if he lost that person he would inevitably feel great pain. He cannot act naturally, because his status demands a certain type of public presentation. He cannot have any friends to confide in, because his ego doesn't allow him to. Friends always come with the implicit threat of betrayal.'

'So even if people look like they have achieved everything, they are actually suffering, isn't that right?'

'Not necessarily. Imagine that same politician has given his soul some leeway. He trusts his friends, he is able to love and he does not expect everybody to betray him immediately.'

'How does he do it?'

'Either he has naturally given his soul space from an early age, or he has been taught by someone in his adulthood, just as I am now teaching you. Status, power and money are only the fruits of a life in which we give space to our soul, so long as we make sure it can manifest itself to the full. Security, attention and certainty are only illusions, and the soul knows that very well. True certainty comes from within. That is why the soul basically does not strain to achieve anything. It is only here and now.'

Tomáš stretched, settled much more comfortably and said, 'It is beginning to make sense. Nobody has explained it to me that way before.'

'It has been presented to you that way all your life, but you have not wanted to see it. You weren't ready for it. The human mind works in a wondrous way. You can program it to only see what you want to see. That is why it is good to use the heart too. It will help you to perceive the truth.'

'How can I tell the difference between somebody who gives space to his soul and somebody who doesn't?'

'Your soul will recognize a connected person. When you learn to give it space again, it will be enough just to ask. However, be careful of these judgements, because you will come to realize in time that all are connected.'

He did not understand, but that didn't particularly bother him. I don't have to understand everything right away, he thought. He preferred to ask about something else:

'You mentioned before that even as children we can connect up with our souls. I suppose this depends on our parents, doesn't it? So what is the right way to bring children up?'

Kohl was very pleased by this question. His eyes lit up and it was with great pleasure that he immediately started explaining:

'The right way for you to bring up children is to have an awakened soul yourself. Your energy will never run out, because it emanates from you and you need never suck it in. The youngster will subconsciously perceive this behaviour and adopt it. Whatever you do, whether good or bad, the child will perceive it and do likewise. If you know what awakens and releases the soul within him, then you naturally give him space so that he can manifest himself fully. A child like that might then feel the occasional lack of attention, certainty and security, but then for most of his childhood he is in contact with his soul, he gives it space and it fills him with an incredible amount of love, energy and hope. The soul itself knows how best to work with the ego, and these children do not very often have problems with disobedience. Of course, they have to go through a period of life when they are ruled by their ego – that is all part of their natural development, but it is not natural at all for them as adults. It does occur, but it definitely should not be that way.'

Tomáš felt touched. 'Thank you very much, Kohl. Nobody has ever explained it to me that way before. Now I understand my sister. Ever since she was little she has wanted to be a figure skater. She spent hours in winter on a nearby lake. Then our parents forbade her, because they were afraid for her, and they didn't have the money for an ice skating rink. This really broke her. I have never again seen her so happy as when she was skating. I had completely forgotten about it. I never realized until we were talking about it just now.'

'My soul is helping yours to recall parts of your life that you had long forgotten. From the ego's viewpoint, they weren't important, but for the soul they were unrepeatable experiences. Yours experienced your sister's sorrow alongside her.'

'Yes, yes! I remember comforting my sister, buying her lollipops and always being close to her. I felt her heartache, but at the same time an enormous sense of thankfulness that we had each other. Strange. I really had forgotten all that.'

'The soul remembers everything. It is directly connected to the souls of others. It is very powerful. It can do unbelievable things if it is free. It is far more powerful than the most highly developed ego, but then it never abuses its powers – it cannot and it does not even want to. Why would it?'

'So when we let it appear, we experience feelings such as love and hope – and we're full of energy. That is what I have been entirely missing lately. So how should I act now? How should I allow it to manifest itself?!' he asked so enthusiastically that he himself was surprised just how carried away he had got.

Kohl looked out of the window. The street was dark – not a soul was to be seen. He glanced at his watch and ended the session for that day.

'We can talk about that next time. In a week if you want.'

'I'd like to. But what am I to do if the feelings of powerlessness and despair come back?'

'Remain connected. The bad feelings won't go away, but you'll be able to put up with them a lot better. Old habits die hard. You'll have to make an effort for quite some time, but later on you'll do it automatically. So long as you are connected to your soul, you'll overcome everything and then you'll be laughing and dancing.'

'But how can you dance when the world around you has gone crazy?' he sighed.

'As I was saying a while ago, we have to learn to live with that burden. So I say we might as well laugh along with it too. Not to worry – you'll learn all that in good time. When things get really bad though, try this.' He put his hairy arm to his mouth and kissed it. He was like a little boy:

'I love myself. I love myself this much. Oh God, how much I love myself.'

'Another joke, eh?'

Kohl shook his head as his face lit up.

'I'm actually being deadly serious here. There is one other point. You have a week before we see each other again. During this time try to open up your mind as much as possible. Imagine that you have been reborn. You can test out the world around you. Try to be like a scientist who believes he is going to find something he did not previously know. Now when you are connected you will see a lot of things differently. What's more, you can squeeze a lot more into an empty vessel than a full one.'

Tomáš didn't understand very much of all this, but again he was not too concerned. He said good-bye to Kohl and set off home, feeling as pleased as if he had just been resurrected. He was overflowing with joy. If he had eaten or drunk anything at Kohl's, he would have suspected him of drugging him. In addition to the euphoria, Tomáš also had an incredibly sharp mind. He reconsidered everything and finally understood why he had been unhappy. He remembered his childhood, and he realized that his father had been manipulating him, his sister and his mother with his questions. But what about those dreams?

Don't you worry about that now, he answered himself, and it sounded like the voice of his intuition. For a long time he had not listened to his intuition, and he was no longer sure now what exactly it sounded like. It occurred to him that his soul manifested itself through his intuition amongst other things.

When he arrived home he immediately embraced Eliška. He wanted to give her at least a little of his happiness. She was quite taken aback, as she hadn't seen him in such a good mood for a long time. After a late supper they chatted together for a while. Tomáš did not have to force himself to speak with his wife. It all rather went of its own accord. Before he fell asleep a thought struck him: I forgot to ask Kohl what he means by that Light.

1/6 Open mind

When Tomáš awoke the next morning he felt well-rested. It had often happened of late that he had slept as much as ten hours and yet still woke up tired. Outside it was raining, and the raindrops drummed on the roof of their attic flat. It sounds very pleasant. I like the sound of rain, he thought. He slowly got out of bed. His lessons didn't start today until nine o'clock, so he had time to eat his breakfast in peace. For the first time in a long time he did not make Eliška's breakfast just out of compulsion.

It was only a twenty minute walk to school, but because it was still raining he preferred to use public transport. Eliška was now driving his car. On the way he got into a state that was similar to the way he was that time he went to the hospital for her. He focused on other people and the impression they were making on him. As he got on the bus, most of the passengers were in a gloomy mood (if it could be called a mood at all), though at the back some children were having a laugh, while next to them two young women were talking animatedly. He decided to go right to the back there. Strange, I feel a lot better here at the back, he thought. It definitely has to do with my visit to Kohl yesterday. For a long time his mind was open, absorbing everything like a sponge.

The children next to him suddenly burst out laughing, which made him laugh too. The young girls started smirking along with him too. Some of the people in the front seats just stared grumpily in their direction, while others settled deeper into their bleak mood, looking like inflated fairground balloons. How very odd, he thought. How come I've never noticed this before?

As he got out he opened up his blue umbrella, which was large enough to encompass another two, and headed for the school at an even pace. For the first time in a long time he was actually happy to be going there. He was looking forward to seeing his pupils and hearing their inquisitive questions, and even to chatting with his colleagues at lunchtime. Monika, an older teacher, often talked about her garden. She spent all her spare time on it in spring and autumn. She replanted the flowers, watered them, fertilized them and tried planting new kinds. She often said the first and the last thing she did every day was to check on her flowers. She lived for them entirely. When she spoke about them her brown eyes were like sparklers. She was very popular at the school both among the teachers and the pupils. Every time Tomáš listened to her, something within him was moved. Now he thought about it he realized that this was the soul within him. And now he was feeling it again!

Honza was sitting in the staff room with her. Now he was into politics. He had even been on the local council for some time. They often got into long political debates. Tomáš liked Honza's pragmatism a lot. He took up various positions on various subjects. Some of his views were rather conservative, while others were liberal. He didn't hold to any particular dogma. He only wanted things to work the way they were supposed to. Because he had his own point of view, he soon came to be something of an inconvenience to the others on the council. When they expected him to support them in a crucial vote he failed to raise his hand. The proposal went against his convictions. After the vote his colleagues just drily informed him he would not get a look in at the council again. And that is the way things turned out. He did not run again. It was a watershed period for Honza, which he found difficult to deal with, but several years had now passed and he had come to terms with it all. The energy and time that he had spent working in local politics were now being channelled elsewhere. He was interested in politics all over the world, and he was trying to find a functioning political system that might work in the circumstances here. He took the Scandinavian countries as his model and kept talking about politicians in Sweden. Tomáš never believed that Honza would ever manage to change anything, but they always had a good chat.

At the grammar school he quickly got into the mad scramble that was always the way there. So many things had to be done. Kohl's view of life had so absorbed him that he decided to present it to 4A. If everybody gave a little leeway to their soul, how would that change the world? he asked himself. Might it not cause more problems than it solved? What if some souls want to harm others? He carried on preparing for his lessons. Eventually he had to acknowledge that he himself did not know all the answers. Better not bring it up in front of the pupils. He never asked them about anything he was not entirely sure of himself. That would reduce his authority. After all, a teacher has to know everything. He observed himself as he arrived at that conclusion. Now he felt worse.

Could that be my ego? he wondered. What if I asked my pupils what they enjoy and what they want to be in life? I won't do any harm that way, and not many people actually ask them about that.

This decision cheered him up, and he felt his soul moving within him again. He promised himself to listen to its wishes more often. He realized that Kohl was right.

When the lesson began there was no stopping him.

'Today I would like to carry out a sociological and psychological survey, with you all taking part. I want you to tell me what you want to do in life. If you don't know then at least let me know what you normally enjoy doing.'

Robert was the first to respond, naturally without putting his hand up.

'What kind of a stupid question is that?'

Lukáš nodded.

'I don't think it's a stupid question,' Dominik retorted. 'I want to be a doctor and save lives.'

'And what makes you say that, Dominik?' Tomáš asked him inquisitively as he sat down at his table. His favourite pupil answered immediately, as if he had been expecting this kind of question all his life.

'When I was small I saw a friend of mine knocked down by a car. All that mayhem and... despair. As soon as a doctor arrived in an ambulance everything changed. The doctor was experienced and very quickly calmed down everyone around by explaining what he was doing. Eventually it all turned out well. I've wanted to be a doctor ever since. I've told my parents and they support me.'

'I want to be a midwife,' Beáta boasted.

Lukáš promptly took this up, adding that he wanted to be a gynaecologist and making the whole class laugh.

Beáta calmly riposted, 'Girls, don't worry. Lukáš is too dumb for that, fortunately for us,' and she turned back to Dominik. 'Maybe we could work together sometime?'

'I hope not. I want to be a surgeon.'

His and Tomáš's lips curled slightly, making another two boys laugh as they understood the joke or at least found it funny.

'And what about you others? What do you want to be? I want you all to answer,' Tomáš challenged the rest of the class.

Almost all 4A had their turn. As the hands of the clock above the blackboard moved further apart, he detected a growing enthusiasm among his pupils. Lenka wanted to be a social worker, Ondra an architect and Kamila a policewoman. 'So the boys respect me,' she added, to her classmates' amusement.

Some of them just did not know, but at least they talked about what they enjoyed: everything from playing the guitar, singing and programming to all kinds of sports, watching TV and going online. The lesson passed very quickly and most of the pupils enjoyed it. Nobody laughed at anybody else because of what they wanted to do or what they enjoyed. When Robert and Lukáš first tried to, he stopped them immediately, and after that they preferred to stay silent.

1/7 Matěj

The next few days passed in a similar vein. Tomáš noticed other people more. He was interested in what his friends, relatives and acquaintances liked doing, and he talked with Eliška considerably more than they were both used to.

Today he was due to go for another session with Kohl. As the week had passed he felt his energy decreasing and again perceived the world more critically. He had quite a few questions to ask. For example, why don't people listen to their souls? His thoughts were disturbed by the white snowflakes which had started to fall for the first time this year. They drifted through the air, in no hurry at all to reach the ground. As if they sensed that they would melt upon impact. He lifted up his jacket collar and walked faster. A couple of minutes later he was happily looking down the main street, with Kohl's office at its end. As always he ran up the stairs, as he did not want to wait for the lift.

He did not expect anybody else to be in the room, but near him there was a ten-year-old boy with what looked like infantile paralysis, sitting in an electric wheelchair. He had short fair hair and thin hands. Kohl was holding a school exercise book, and when he saw Tomáš's surprised expression he welcomed him with a smile:

'Hi, Tom, good to see you again. This is Matěj. He's going to help us with the next lesson. We've just been learning some chemistry. You don't mind if we finish later, do you?' He looked towards the boy, who answered with a smile and body language typical of the disabled:

'I don't like studying very much. It's all so boring. Is Tom the new friend you have been talking about, Kohl?'

'Yes, he is. What has your last week been like then? I'm very interested,' Kohl asked as he placed the dog-eared exercise book on the table.

Tomáš briefly described his entire week, focusing mainly on the changes in his thinking and behaviour – the way he now noticed other people's souls more. He spoke about the lesson spent on the wishes of the soul and about his improved mood. 'I have a couple of questions too!'

'I am pleased to see you are beginning to listen to your soul. Your mind is also now open. Remember what is useful and let the useless go. And what do you want to ask?'

Tomáš frowned for a while, as he visibly pondered the best formulation:

'So what is the ego actually good for? Wouldn't it be better just to get rid of it completely? Why don't people listen to their souls? And also, what did you mean when you spoke of the Light?'

Both of his companions' faces lit up with a broad smile. Kohl did not conceal his enthusiasm.

'I have not met anybody as inquisitive as you for quite a long time, Tom. You think up questions that most people would not even dream of. At the same time you clearly want to hear an honest answer. It really is important for you to hear the truth.'

Tomáš blushed, but Kohl did not notice:

'The ego is an excellent servant, but a bad master. It wants to gain control over people, all the world and all situations. It wants to be the untrammelled ruler of everything. It demands and expects profit, but feels no compassion. Why don't we just get rid of it completely? In the first place we cannot and in any case it wouldn't do us any good. Our aim is to get it onto our side, so that it works for us rather than the other way round. Your ego is a part of you. Why would you want to get rid of a part of yourself? Without our egos we would be unable to understand other people who are governed by their egos. And we would often not have sufficient motivation to do anything. There is nothing wrong in wanting to win if you know it's only a game. The ego is what keeps you going when your strength is draining away and your tongue is hanging out down to the ground. It is also a source of critical thinking. It is frequently suspicious and finds pretexts in everything. We do not actually live in a world where you can trust everybody and the ego can reveal when somebody wants to outwit you. So why get rid of it? Make it your best friend. Always be close to it, and try to meet its wishes, if your soul agrees to them. That is perfect symbiosis. Like a wise old man who knows the world, and a young man who has the feeling the world belongs to him. As a young man you have a problem thinking things through, and as an old man you have a problem acting spontaneously. Combine them. Now what was your other question?'

'Oh I think you're right. Thanks for the explanation. But then why do people not listen to their soul when it is of such benefit?'

'I am always right,' he joked. 'Though recently my memory has been getting a bit worse.'

Quick as a flash Tomáš interjected, 'That comes of all that smoking,' which made everybody in the room laugh. When Kohl caught his breath, he answered that question too.

'I like your sense of humour, Tom. People don't listen to their soul, because they have not yet been shown that that is what has to be done. Most parents can only acquire energy from others, so that is what they teach their children. As soon as enough people understand the game being played by their ego, they release themselves from it and begin to listen to their soul. Then the world makes a quantum leap.'

'Is it not always going to be that way though? I thought the world had worked like that since time out of mind.'

'You're right that it has been working like that for a long time, but it is going to change soon. More about that some other time. Now here we have a distinguished guest!' And he looked smilingly at Matěj, who returned his smile.

'Matěj and his lesson today are ultimately connected with your last question. Some people are born and find themselves with a tremendous gift. They can light up the darkest place with their soul. Matěj is one of these people. He is pure light. His ego has practically no power at all over him. He listens to his soul and he is able to raise the energy level of people around him to an amazing degree. Did you notice when you first started listening to your soul that you started to glow, and people around you automatically started looking better? For example, the children in your class and the passengers in that bus? People who are connected not only have sufficient energy for themselves, but they also radiate it all around them. These people are the light. Just like Matěj here. His parents brought him here for me to help him. It didn't take me long to realize that he is doing perfectly fine. I understood that it was his parents who needed help. He has a very unique energy system. Every time I see him, something about him surprises me. Something I did not see previously. It's all very complex, but suffice it to say that Matěj constantly radiates energy, call it love if you will. Constantly. Under any conditions. He is perfect. Unfortunately, his parents still see him as afflicted,' Kohl concluded with a sigh.

Matěj then entered the discussion, moving his head up and down as he spoke.

'When I was growing up I felt I was in a bad dream. Everyone kept arguing and trying to harm others. No one understood anyone else. They are all such marvellous beings and yet they argue like that, put each other down and hurt each other. I thought there was something wrong with me, because I was different. Fortunately I met Kohl here, and he explained everything to me. The main thing is that he understands the way I look at the world. I do like him a lot,' and he looked at Kohl. His eyes were glowing so much, Tomáš found it quite unbelievable.

Tomáš's eyes moistened as he realized just how often he deprived people of their energy even though they did not deserve it, and how often instead of providing words of comfort and hope he only hammered in another nail in their coffin, not only in the case of outsiders, but also family members. Suddenly it all came home to him and he felt ashamed. He remembered being involved in bullying a classmate at school. Tomáš and his friends often stole Martin's lunch and made fun of him. He and the boys took it as a bit of fun, but Martin suffered as a result. They knew this but never admitted it to themselves. Now he finally realized. Martin had a light similar to that of Matěj. Now he saw everything from his standpoint. I used to treat that kind of light cruelly, he thought. He wanted to be swallowed up by the earth, while at the same time he felt great relief.

Kohl was well aware of these emotions.

'You see how Matěj works so marvellously? Now you know how pure love works. I see that your energy system has got rid of some of its blocks.'

'Energy system? What is that? Do you see it?' Tomáš implored, feeling like a little boy whose mum was explaining how the world worked, but who still did not know enough.

'I shall explain it to you in simple terms – you operate like a battery. Your soul charges you up and your ego runs you down. It doesn't matter if your ego is running down somebody else or yourself. As I say, there is nothing wrong with that. You don't throw your computer out of the window just because it has consumed electricity. The more your soul manages to charge you up, the higher the frequency that you have. The higher the frequency you have, the more love and energy you can pass on. If your body or mind is broken or blocked, then your energy level is reduced. You only see the worst side of things and you miss out on the best side. You also feel tired, because your body is working with less energy than it is used to. Imagine it like damaged cells in a battery.'

'So I can solve all my problems by increasing my energy levels?'

'No. You won't solve your problems that way. You will only get to a higher frequency and see the problem as an opportunity, because every "problem" is actually an opportunity to understand something, but in order to understand it you must have enough energy. If you realize that you are connected to everything and with everything, you will always have enough energy.'

'Hold on, Kohl, I am getting a bit confused here,' and Tomáš sat up straight. After a moment of reflection he added:

'So the only thing I have to do is raise my energy level? This has something to do with my soul, doesn't it?'

'Exactly! If you are connected then you will always know what to do,' and then Matěj joined in the discussion.

'We really have the power to create a heaven on earth here. Find the most beautiful idea of yourself within yourself and then follow it unconditionally. Radiate as much love as you are able to. Make your life something unusual. Let your soul show itself to the full. Give out love everywhere you go, and never ask what you will get back for it. Even if you feel bad, give it out. Hate only deprives you of energy. Life is too short for you not to love. Love overcomes all obstacles – love always knows the way forward – love never loses hope. Love makes life life. Love shows you that you are alive. If you do not love then you are not alive,' and he supported himself in his powerchair in order to lean forward. 'If you feel bad, ask your soul what needs to be done. All you need to do is to fill yourself with love and start listening to your soul. That is the only way to find out that your soul, your highest self, your highest conception of yourself, is speaking... The god within you... The light within you will lead you and guide your way, even through the darkest place.'

The way he spoke threw Tomáš totally off balance. Just a while back he was a disabled person, dependent on the help of others, but he had just shown Tomáš this great and pure truth. He looked at him in admiration and asked in a quivering voice, 'What am I to do if I lack energy?'

'It's good to stroke a cat, take a walk in the woods, dance, paint, run, help others or basically do anything that gives you the feeling you're enjoying life. That is food for the soul.'

He wanted to know more. 'And how do those lights work?'

This time it was Kohl who answered. 'Higher frequency energy awakens higher frequencies in yourself. When you remember this frequency, you can create it yourself. All it takes is for somebody like Matěj here to show you that it is possible. That it is possible to love people regardless of how they appear on the surface. He looks straight into their soul.'

'Hold on! If I understand well, I have to look for higher frequencies. That does not necessarily mean looking for people like Matěj, because his is so high, he can perceive the high frequencies within ordinary people. For Matěj everybody is light...'

'That's it!' Kohl exclaimed, and Matěj expressed his pleasure alongside him. Kohl then added: 'You have grasped an amazingly important lesson. Remember that the higher the energy you give out, the higher the energy you perceive and the higher the energy you have again. It is like a spiral. It works that way downwards too. Because you have recently felt bad, you stopped giving. Now your energy system is in total order. It will grow naturally and increase its capacity. As time goes by you will feel better and better, both physically and mentally.'

'And how long will it keep increasing?'

This time Matěj answered, 'The soul has no limits.'

And Kohl added, 'Limits are an invention of the ego. The increase in energy will accelerate your development. The more energy you learn to take from within, the less you will need it from others. After that you will no longer think about what others can give you, and what you require from others, but what you can offer them. Connect to the source directly and you will see what it does to you. Simply learn to give a bit more. It is just a matter of habit. Get used to being connected all the time.'

Again Tomáš felt his soul moving within him. It whispered: Put your heart into everything you do. He asked: 'Can I make myself love somebody this way?'

Matěj sensed what he was asking about:

'I think you're talking about your wife. What's her name?'

He was quite surprised at how he had guessed right, and just nodded: 'Eliška.'

'What a lovely name. If you try too hard it doesn't usually work. The more you actually try, the worse it gets. When everything is moving upwards then you no longer impede its course, and everything gets sorted out by itself. Perhaps not the way you want it, but in a way that is better for you both. Imagine Eliška, cut through all the constricting bonds between you and start afresh. But I think I can set your mind at rest. Your relationship is all right now. You just need to show it at a physical level, and this might take some time.'

It was all Tomáš could do to refrain from bursting out crying with happiness. He felt so good now! He had such an appetite for life! He could not recall ever having experienced anything like that before. It had not been so intensive even at their last meeting. After a period of silence the discussion continued, as they chatted about how to distinguish the voice of the soul from the voice of the ego. As always, Kohl knew the answer.

'The soul manifests itself through inspiration. The ego through pressure and stress. If you are in your heart then you will distinguish those voices, and you will act with clarity and certainty.'

They then helped Matěj with his studies, chatted about his parents and grandparents and what he was going to do when he grew up. He fidgeted in his powerchair as he daydreamed:

'When I grow up I'm going to be a diplomat and bring together opposing nations and religions.'

And this was the first time in Tomáš's life that he had believed someone with his heart, not his mind.

It was time to say goodbye. Kohl told him that the sessions were over. 'You won't go under again! You don't need me any more.'

Tomáš felt that way too. Still, they agreed to see each other as friends. They had plenty to tell each other. As he was leaving, Tomáš could not help but give Matěj a hug. It was a little unusual to embrace someone in a powerchair, but it was very pleasant. On the way home he considered the entire affair. His appetite for life had returned. He wanted to get back to sorting out his problems and challenges. He promised himself to always listen to his soul when it came to important matters.

His thoughts then turned towards old age. He had never looked forward to it. It struck him as all too painful, all that talk about illness and death. Now he told himself that being old did not have to be so awful. Providing he looked after his mental health, he would be physically all right too. He could devote himself to his hobbies, travel and educating himself. Suddenly he felt a switch in his mind had been flipped. What had once been a notion had dissolved, leaving only the truth behind. More and more needless old views evaporated away on his way home, leaving behind the pure essence, the pure truth. Why didn't all this occur to me before!? he wondered.

1/8 A fulfilled life

About a month had passed since Tomáš started regularly attending Kohl's sessions, when he came home to find Eliška at the kitchen table. Her make-up was tear-smudged and she looked very upset.

'What's the matter, dear?' he asked, but she did not reply. After a moment of silence she exploded, bawling and yelling. 'I know you have a lover. I know it! You've completely changed. You're always smiling. You're all happy and young again!'

This completely took him aback. He did not know how to respond to this accusation. He felt as if handcuffs had just been slapped on him, and he was now being read his rights. You have the right to remain silent. Anything you say may be taken down and used in evidence against you.

He had lately been spending more and more time with Kohl, so he had always told her he had to stay behind at school. It never occurred to him that she would take it this way. Now he regretted not telling her the truth. Eliška had been suffering in silence over it. She was really angry and in tears. He could barely recognize this face of hers. He was surprised at just how much anger she had stowed away inside her. She must have been suppressing it for quite some time. He tried to deal with it from the position of an observer as Kohl had taught him, saying to himself: Have I really been that way? That is exactly what the domination of fear and the ego looks like. After some time she calmed down and stopped pushing him away.

Tomáš embraced her, apologized for being dishonest and explained everything. She had her doubts for a while, but eventualy came round. It was then that he realized what a beautiful face she had. All her features combined to form the unique shape of her face. She was so attractive. He agreed to take her along with him to meet Kohl soon, and from that time on their relationship was on a completely different footing.

The accusation of infidelity made Kohl laugh out loud. He summed it up this way:

'I have never yet been anybody's lover.'

'There's a first time for everything.'

'Very true.'

'What bothers me, my friend, is how much you're smoking these days.'

Today they were both sitting on the carpet and Kohl was happily puffing away. As always he answered in an affable manner.

'My friend, you take care of your own addictions,' and he choked.

'I hope you're not going to toke away like that in front of Eliška. She's coming with me next week.'

'What? Are you afraid I might make a bad impression?' and he put on his most serious expression.

Tomáš changed the subject.

'Do you think money can corrupt people?'

'Money doesn't corrupt people. People are corrupted by their own stupidity.'

He thought about this for a while. He did not know many wealthy people.

Generally accepted opinions are not always right, he thought as he looked at his teacher happily finishing his joint. He gave Kohl a hug from the side.

'I've been doing a lot better since we have known each other. Even my backache has stopped.'

'Because you have cast off a lot of ballast.'

'A religious colleague of mine asked if I've converted.'

'What did you say?'

'The truth, that is, I don't like the church, but I do believe in something.'

'Have you noticed that a lot of people criticize the church, but nobody criticizes Jesus Christ?'

'That's true. What do you think of Jesus, Kohl?'

'I think they all took him too seriously. I think that often when he was alone on the Mount, he used to dance, and when he got talking with his disciples he was often smiling. I think he enjoyed his time spent in brothels with criminals and prostitutes. He didn't take it as a duty or an attempt to correct them, as is often said. I think that he really loved these people and liked to talk with them, without being particularly bothered about what they were like.'

'True love performs miracles. Do you think anybody will ever manage to destroy Jesus's legacy?'

'I'm an optimist. The Catholic Church has tried to do so for two thousand years and still hasn't succeeded.'

Both of them started to laugh, then Kohl grew serious.

'Of course the world is not black and white. If we had to describe it the way it really is, we'd be forced to remain silent.'

After pondering this idea for a couple of minutes Tomáš asked, 'How did you get it anyway?'

'Some friends bring it me from Holland. Very high-quality merchandise. Want to try some?'

Tomáš shook his head. 'No, not that. How did you arrive at everything you've been telling me about. It's not exactly general knowledge.'

'Oh that,' Kohl laughed, acting dumb. Tomáš now knew him only too well, so he clearly saw he was pulling his leg. Kohl knew what he'd been asking all along.

'I studied psychology at university. I was one of the top students at the Faculty. I thought I'd go into practice after graduating, but the old regime found me an inconvenience, so I ended up working at an out-of-the-way warehouse. After the revolution I took off for the Amazon rainforest, where I lived with this tribe for ten years. I learnt most of what I know now from the local shaman. After I came back to civilization it was difficult for me to get used to having to pay for everything. I spent several more years on the street. But don't worry, I definitely wasn't badly off. We don't need anything at all to be happy. You know that for yourself. I learnt a lot at the time and got to know some amazing people. Only then did I understand it was time to open a psychology practice. You know that feeling when you often consider something, but you know that now is not the right time. Then it all suddenly clicks together in your heart and mind, and you go for it. It was difficult at first, but I was good, so people kept recom-

mending me.'

Tomáš attempted to express how much he appreciated him. 'Well, thank you for everything, my friend.'

Kohl took a drink of water, as his throat was dry after his long talk and, of course, his joint. He did not answer, but a smile appeared on his wrinkled face, which communicated everything that was needed. His eyes were full of life and wisdom. They flashed as another ques- tion occurred to him. 'How would you define unconditional love?'

'One time I said some awful things to my mum. This hurt her a lot, and we didn't speak to each other for about a week. Then I realized what an idiot I'd been. I went to their place to apologize to her. She wasn't expecting an apology at all, but gave me a hug and asked me if I'd stay for supper. A couple of years later we were chatting about it, and you know what she said to me about it? Nothing you ever do will stop you from being my son.'

— • —

The meeting between Tomáš, Eliška and Kohl was very pleasant. Kohl told more jokes than usual and spent most of the time talking about what a fulfilled life meant for him. For Tomáš this was nothing new. Eliška was quite stunned, but appreciative. On the way home they got talking about what an amazing person Kohl was.

'Well, I'm glad that my lover made such a good impression on you,' Tomáš smirked.

'Hey, that's not fair. What was I supposed to think?' and she stole his cap.

When they got home they again made love. This had recently been quite frequent and always totally amazing.

Before he fell asleep, various thoughts shot through his mind. In everybody's life there comes a time when we realize why we were born

– a moment when everything becomes clear to us. This had just happened to him now – and he was so glad that it had not waited until his deathbed. When he occasionally observed other people he could tell how they felt. Sometimes it was enough just to look at someone and he felt better immediately. It was amazing. He had become something greater. He felt so good. Those voices telling him he was a wreck and that he would never amount to anything had finally disappeared.

Most people yearn so much to travel and see the world without ever seeing at least a reflection of the beauty of the world that we each have within us, he sighed. That was why at school he had stopped focusing on teaching his pupils facts, but took care to make sure they understood the contexts and why things happened the way they did. He was also no longer afraid to be hard on his pupils when they needed it, though he only did that when he was sure it would benefit them. He had learnt to be what people needed. He was someone different for each individual, and yet he was still himself. As if he had suddenly grown up and taken in a lot more of everything. It was an amazing feeling. He felt this enormous self-confidence and yet at the same time a deep humility towards life, even though things were by no means ideal. Tomáš and his best friend Ondra had grown rather apart and no longer got on so well. It was with these feelings that he fell asleep.

— • —

At the weekend the Jedličkas went out to enjoy themselves – to a dance for the first time in a long time. They went along with a gang of friends they had in common. They all had a marvellous time. When Tomáš danced to his favourite song, his soul was to be heard: *Dance as if nobody was looking. Enjoy the fact you can be together with Eliška and your friends. It is not everybody who has that good fortune.* As the individual notes passed through his body he realized how music brought people together. Whatever opinions and religions they might have, music made it all the same. It actually is all the same. All the same! Dancing is just another form of meditation, he realized, and he pictured Jesus, dancing upon the Mount. He then relinquished all thoughts and just danced.

A week later they went on holiday to Paris. This was a fifth wedding anniversary present from the family. As he watched his wife walking along the Seine, she struck him as very attractive and beautiful. Her long legs, narrow waist and round bottom fit nicely into her dark-blue jeans, while she wore a chic scarf around her neck, round which her straight fair hair fell. Her velvet complexion was illuminated by the street lamps, her small mouth with the bewitching lips was slightly open, and best of all were her large brown tear-shaped eyes, which he could stare into for hours on end. He could scarcely believe that not so long ago she had looked unattractive. It is strange how my surroundings change as I do, he thought.

1/9 Freedom

This was now the best period ever in Tomáš's life. Every lesson at school was something special. He often took up several simple points from Kohl's lessons and discussed them with his pupils. Today they were talking about freedom. To start the lesson he said, 'Do you have the impression that you're free? How can you actually tell?'

The first to respond was Beáta. 'When I used to help out with the dishes or the vacuuming as a youngster, I really enjoyed doing it, until my mum told me I had to. Then I lost all my enthusiasm and I only did it very reluctantly.'

'It's like that with me,' Lukáš piped up, adding, 'the more I'm forced to do something, the less I give a damn,' and he smiled. He had been quite different of late. He wasn't as unruly, and he got more involved in debates. Then again, Robert was still the same, if not worse.

Dominik raised his hand. 'We all do things best when we decide to do them freely. And what do we freely decide on? Well, most probably what we like doing best. What fulfils us.'

Tomáš agreed. 'What's best for children? A happy divorced parent, or unhappy parents who are still together with them? Is it more important to have a well-paid job that eats you up inside, or a job that you find fulfilling with a smaller salary? You can all answer that for yourselves and you'll know from the answer whether or not you're free. Do you find social status and security to be more important? Then you are living in a personal prison with high fences. Are you going to do what you enjoy and what you find expressive at any cost? Then you are free. Congratulations.'

His pupils had recently become accustomed to the way he spoke so wisely, but someone could always be found to express surprise.

'Well, I like the way you're always coming out with this great wisdom. Where do you get it all from?' asked Mirka.

Lukáš never put his hand up on principle when he wanted to say anything: 'My dad's a prison warder. What he tells me about his work makes it pretty clear to me that sometimes you have to restrict other people's freedom.'

'You are right, Lukáš. Good point. But then your freedom can only be restricted if you endanger yourself or somebody else,' Tomáš answered.

Dominik hit the nail on the head: 'But then isn't that abused by various dictators? They tell people they're being protected, but that's just a hypocritical cover for their regime, so they don't lose hold on power.'

Tomáš nodded: 'I do agree, but then a totalitarian regime is not really a good example to take when we are talking about freedom. A democracy should be able to operate by giving you the opportunity to defend yourself, so that society can impartially judge your arguments, but of course we're running ahead of ourselves a little here. We won't be having politology until next semester,' he smiled, as he got back to the original subject. 'We're all responsible for ourselves. If you feel it's right to limit somebody else's rights so that he does no more harm, then do please go ahead, but careful! Only very exceptionally! Just like police officers do when they take a drunken driver's car keys, or a court that locks up criminals, so they don't pose a danger to themselves and those around them. Or when they give you a sedative at hospital, so you don't move and hurt yourself.'

Lukáš remained unconvinced. 'But if everybody does what they want, won't it end up in anarchy?'

A quiet descended on the class, which was not broken until Tomáš spoke up. 'No, it won't, because there is this catch: To be free we have to follow certain rules. A nice paradox, eh?'

The pupils just stared at him dumbstruck, so he immediately explained himself.

'How can we be free if we don't have enough discipline to get rid of our addictions? And believe me, we all have our addictions – even I do. The more we free ourselves from our addictions, the freer we will be. It is a simple equation.'

Dominik took advantage of this opportunity. 'Well, I'm quite dependent on my mum. How am I supposed to free myself from her?'

This made the entire class laugh. Other pupils started bringing up their addictions to different kinds of food, computers, the internet and various social networks, as well as masturbation, which Robert did not neglect to bring up. The lesson passed quickly. It struck Tomáš as amusing that he sat on the carpet before Kohl as a pupil and novice, learning the absolute basics about his soul, whereas in front of his pupils it was his turn to be the seasoned teacher.

After lunch the 4A pupils were waiting for a photograph session. Even though he was not their class teacher they insisted he should be in the photo too, and after some persuasion he agreed. As he was then going back to the staff room, he managed to catch Libor, the care-taker. He had noticed that one of the urinals in the toilets was not work-ing, so he wanted to report it. He knocked on the door.

'There comes a time in the life of every caretaker when somebody tells him that a urinal in the toilet on the second floor is not working. And your time has now come.'

'Well, Tom, I just wonder if you'll still be in a good mood when I ask you to help me fix it,' Libor could not resist saying.

Tomáš bent back to catch hold of his loins:

'Ouch, my back, again. I'm going back to the staff room to lie down.'

His relations with his colleagues had also improved, with the ex-ception of Karel, who was always the same. If anything it was even worse with him, as he probably envied Tomáš his growing popu-larity. Still he didn't worry his head much about that. Kohl had ad-vised him to focus as little as possible on Karel, and so not to add any energy to the conflict.

In the staff room he met up with Honza, with whom he immediat-ely got talking. Today Honza was talking about why the smart and the not so smart pupils should be in the same classroom. He wasn't happy that some private schools only accepted the most talented chil-dren. Tomáš agreed with him. He knew very well that intelligence without a heart is good for nothing.

As Honza was pouring his tea, he changed the subject:

'Have you read that interview with Novotný? About his attacks on women in politics? He reckons they ought to stay home cooking and washing.'

'If there were more women in politics, the deputies in parliament wouldn't argue so much and would listen to each other more. This way they just compete over who's going to get the most votes for their policy, and they don't try to come to an agreement over anything that would suit them all.'

'Well, exactly. What's more, politics would be more open, and there would be more to actually look at, if you know what I mean.' Both burst out laughing. Then Honza continued:

'If people focused more on the welfare of everybody, and not just on their own interests, we could introduce the kind of direct democracy that I've been considering.'

'And what is that?' Tomáš put down the pen that he was going to use to mark some tests.

'Imagine certain professional groups, for example IT specialists and teachers. Each group will always include people that understand their subject both in theory and practice. When there's a vote on laws concerning a particular group, then that particular group would have to pass them. Each one from the comfort of their own home on the internet. This would ensure that bills are no longer decided upon by politicians who know nothing about them. It would also speed up the passage of these bills and save a lot of money.'

'That's an excellent idea, but how would you be able to tell who has the right to decide a particular law?'

'Ah, I've thought about that as well. You would have to meet certain conditions, either involving education or experience,' Honza answered with a sparkle in his eyes.

'Well, it's a very good model, but it would require some development in political thinking. People in each group would have to decide for the benefit of everybody and not just for their own group. At the same time a system like that would have to enjoy general confidence and support. Voting on the final form of the bill would have to include all citizens, and important amendments would also have to be approved by everybody.'

'I haven't thought it all through like that yet. You've broadened my horizons there, thanks. Now we just need to make people think of everybody's welfare when they're making decisions,' Honza sighed.

'Well, what you have described there is just a kind of outline, but all great things come from a simple idea. Do work on it. I think it'll be worth the effort. You might be able to write a book on it eventually.'

'Thanks for the support. It might well work out that way.'

'Is that kind of idea meant to be left-wing or right-wing?' Tomáš wondered, while already half-guessing the answer.

Honza, who was just throwing his teabag into the waste basket, answered:

'A bit of both. For example, in Sweden they have a left-wing government that rules responsibly without incurring debts, while in Greece it was actually the right that built up a pile of debt. In principle it's best if people have certain basics for free, without any effort. That is an element of communism. Of course, people do not appreciate what they have for free, so anything above the standard would be paid for.'

Tomáš asked with his mouth full: 'And what are those basics?'

'Basic food, housing and education. Nobody should be afraid that if they're unemployed they'll go hungry or lose the roof over their head. If you want more, such as a car, or to have a beer with friends or go on holiday with your wife, then you have to work.'

'Okay fine, but if you don't have to work then who's going to do those jobs that nobody wants to do, on a factory conveyor belt, for example?'

'Robots and computers. Factories like that are already in existence these days. They're proving to be economically very viable, and there's no lack of machines for standard operations. What's more, when you add up the overall costs, machines are a lot cheaper. As artificial intelligence keeps developing, robots are becoming more and more able to do most conveyor-belt work.'

'I'm not so keen on that model. It's still something of a utopia these days. If people didn't have to work then most of them wouldn't.'

'Unfortunately,' and the sparks dimmed in Honza's eyes.

'Still,' Tomáš raised his eyebrows, 'if people began to listen to their inner feelings more and to do what they enjoy in life and what works for them, then I can imagine it working. Take into account that a lot of us make a living doing what we don't enjoy. As soon as enough people realize they don't have to make a living doing what they don't enjoy...' and he fell silent for a while.

'As soon as they realize they can do what they most enjoy, and as a result, what most fulfils them, then they will be happy,' and again he mused, this time with his eyes closed. 'As soon as we mature as a society, your model could work and will do! The system needs to be changed, so that we all make a living doing what fulfils us and thus what contributes most to society.'

Honza's eyes were sparkling again. 'Can I ask you something, Tom?'

'Sure.'

'How come you're so different these days. You smile much more. You're far more balanced and calm, and you look a lot healthier. Our discussions don't end up in arguments and misunderstandings, like they used to. What's happened to you?'

'Well, I've realized I don't have as many problems as I thought I had, and I created most of them myself anyway. I didn't appreciate life and all that it brings enough. Now things are better. I'm happy for what I have.'

Honza stood up and quickly drank up his tea.

'Must run for my lesson!'

— • —

The school year was over so Tomáš and Eliška had a lot more time for each other. They laughed a lot together and often made love. The night was clear and it was pleasantly warm outside. He came back from the veranda into the chalet, gazing at his attractive wife. She reciprocated his loving gaze, her brown eyes shining in the glow of flames from the fireplace, so sincere and pure. He stroked her hair and embraced her for a long time. Then he again stared into her eyes and kissed her. When their lips touched, he felt so much energy coursing between them.

Tomáš had the impression he was touching her for the first time in his life. He began to stroke her, as she did with him. Soon they were passionately kissing. Their quiet groans were occasionally counterpointed by the crackling of the fire. The closer they came to the moment of joining, the fewer the thoughts that passed through his mind. At length he submerged entirely in the present moment and instinctively stroked and stimulated Eliška in just the right places to excite her the most. And she reciprocated. As they conjoined, the world stood still. Such moments were so complete and experienced absolutely in the present. He observed her perfect face and rejoiced, feeling a flush of energy and love at each kiss. The excitement grew. It was something astonishing, something magnificent!

The more he tried to make sure she liked it, the more he liked it himself. She returned all the energy he gave her, adding her own. That way the energy kept circulating and increasing between them until there was a gigantic explosion that could only be likened to a supernova. Tomáš was filled with a heavenly peace as he felt reborn. A thought flashed through his mind: If only this feeling could last forever. They looked at each other, and Eliška wiped his perspiring brow. They did not have to say anything, as both of them knew it was their best lovemaking ever. After a couple of minutes they fell asleep, their arms and legs intertwined, as a single being.

1/10 Important news

Tomáš became accustomed to succeeding at everything. When he had described his recent progress to his teacher-cum-friend, Kohl responded with a smile.

'These are just the fruits of a life lived in harmony with your soul.'

Today they were going to see each other again. It was hot, and he could hardly breathe in the bus. Most of the people around him were perspiring and tired. He squeezed out past them and walked down a few yards to the building where Kohl had his office. As always they talked first about what they had been doing over the previous week, and then Kohl grew a little more serious.

'So how come you've stopped talking to some of the people you know, who are at a lower level?'

'Like a lower energy level? Well, I've understood that the kind of people we mix with most are the ones we are most like. I only want to mix with people who can give me something, to move a little higher again, you see?'

'I once made the same mistake in life. I thought that I was so far forward that I wasn't making any more mistakes. When I met someone, a couple of words was all it took for me to be able to say what they were missing and what they needed to change in themselves. I wasn't mistaken either, except in one respect, and unfortunately for me this was the biggest mistake I have ever made.'

'And what was that?'

'I'd forgotten that I'm a human being just like anybody else and that other people do not have to change in any way in order to come up to my yardstick of perfection. I did not realize that I should like myself and others just as we are. Then one evening it dawned on me. I was able to imagine what I would do in their situation. It occurred to me that I ought to provide them with support and love, so they could make decisions as well as they were able, but not to force my own decision-making on them. Life isn't just a series of meetings with erudite people, who are highly knowledgeable and don't make any mistakes. It's not a matter of discussing what the world should be like with them. That is just fine, but for me life is basically about helping people who have lost their way to find it back to themselves again. Not just to talk about what the world should look like, but to actually change it. Whenever I forget that, life gives me a little kick to help me remember.'

Tomáš felt rather put down as he answered:

'But why should I force myself to mix with people I have nothing to say to?'

'Nobody wants that of you. Just don't go thinking that your way is the only way. You should be humble all the time,' Kohl put his hand to his heart, 'and express respect for the ways that others have chosen. I forgot to do that. You have the opportunity to learn from my mistake. It doesn't always have to be your own mistakes that help you to realize something.'

'Well, I don't understand. I don't think I'm doing anything wrong. You don't have to understand everything more than I do,' Tomáš snapped and immediately regretted it. Now he expected Kohl to pull him up a little, but instead the latter just quietly responded:

'You are being quite logical. That's fine, but it's not the reason I like you so much. When I first got to know you, there was something about you that impressed me, and this has grown over time.'

'And what was that?' Tomáš asked apologetically.

'You are very much in your heart. You often act in a way that's illogical to an outside observer, but you listen to your heart. This doesn't bring about any results, at least not visible ones, but it does shed some light. A lot of people that I have known for years know this world very well. They understand it perfectly, but they're unable to be in their hearts as you are. What we've been talking about – try to think it over a little at home, but this time with your heart. Because we can only see properly with our heart.'

Tomáš still wasn't convinced he had made a mistake at all. He treated everybody with respect – he just no longer got along that well with some old friends. Kohl looked him straight in the eye with a wise and kindly expression as always:

'I was beginning to worry you might obey every word I say. I'm glad you have your own mind.'

Tomáš did not respond to this at all. When his friend saw he was feeling down he asked:

'So what's up then, Tom?'

'I get pissed off by some people's hypocrisy and spinelessness. They'll tell you one thing to your face and say something else about you behind your back. Or they'll change their opinions as it suits them. They act like your best friend and betray you behind your back!'

'You have to treat life with a certain detachment, Tom. It's not everyone who has your good fortune, or who gets as much out of life as you do.'

'Well, now I get the feeling I haven't learnt that much from you over the last six months.'

Kohl put on the face that he always put on when he realized how he could help someone – he wrinkled his brow and opened his wise eyes wide:

'When you get up in the morning do you feel that spark? Or do you have the feeling that you're commuting to and from work like a zombie? Do you look at the world around you or are you blind? Does your life have any meaning or doesn't it?'

Tomáš took a deep breath:

'I want my life to make sense, but I don't know if I'm going to succeed in that.'

'I've always very much appreciated your honesty, my dear friend, but your life is not always going to make sense. Still, if you honestly and steadfastly seek the essence of everything, accept the good and reject the evil, then your life will never lose meaning. It isn't a question of how long you're going to be in this world, but how you're going to make use of your time here.'

The corners of Tomáš's mouth finally lifted. 'Thank you, my friend.'

— • —

A few days later he was going home from school when he received a text message from Eliška:

'Come home right now.'

This threw him completely off balance, and he quickened his pace to get back to her as soon as he could. He was hoping against hope that nothing bad had happened to her. He remembered her father, who had been having heart problems of late, and tried to calm himself: I'm sure nothing has happened to him, he thought. He unlocked the door with slightly shaking hands, behind which Eliška was waiting for him. She leapt on him straight away:

'I'm pregnant! God, I'm pregnant!'

'Wha-at?!' Tomáš exclaimed. 'When? How? The doctor said we couldn't...' he stammered.

'It was that time at the chalet. I don't know how, but it happened. I'm so happy! I love you.'

'I love you too!' and he kissed her. Tears streamed down their faces.

Then he joked: 'We'll have to take advantage well in advance, because after Jonáš is born, we'll be going twenty years without proper sex.'

'She'll be called Věrka!' Eliška countered.

The afternoon then belonged to them alone. They lay side by side, wordlessly gazing at each other and completely forgetting about time. He had the feeling he had just fallen in love with her. Eliška felt the same way. Their brows touched and they stroked each other tenderly. He again regretted not having fully appreciated her beauty for so long. He could not now imagine a more beautiful and gracious mum for his child or a more wonderful wife. They embraced and enjoyed the present moment. Everything else came to a halt. The two of them had not met by chance. He felt their souls were conjoined, complementing each other and to some extent merging together. He realized as he drew near that nothing else on earth smelled so wonderful. He adored that fragrance. He loved to fall asleep beside her. He wanted every day to end that way for the rest of his life.

— • —

As he announced this happy news, Kohl listened attentively. Tomáš told him how they had been trying unsuccessfully to conceive a child for eighteen months. They had visited a specialist, who told them the sad news:

'You can't have a child. Your sperm has insufficient mobility.'

Tomáš ended his story with a joke: 'It strikes me as a miracle, presuming of course that it is my child!'

'Of course that is always a miracle! Just like every conception and birth. The doctors don't know everything. Every day hundreds of things come to light that scientists and doctors had no clue about. That's all part of human evolution. You mustn't believe everything they say,' and Kohl took another toke.

When he told Honza the next day, he literally fell off his chair.

'What? A baby? I knew you both wanted one, and you hadn't pulled it off for a long time. Congratulations, mate!'

'Thanks, Honza,' he said helping him up from the floor. 'I told you not to rock your chair like that.'

1/11 Kohl's family

I t had rained almost non-stop for the previous two weeks, and everywhere was waterlogged. A strong wind had been blowing since early morning, carrying away the vast clouds, as huge as an entire city. When the sun finally broke through from behind them, Tomáš went out for a walk in the park. He had never liked the autumn, as everything dried up and perished, but this year for the first time he noticed how beautiful and colourful it all was. Every autumn carries within it the promise of the following spring. The leaves rustled pleasantly underfoot.

Again he began to notice how many nice people were living around and mixing with him. He realized that some of them were awakened, others were still waking and yet others were sound asleep. As he was going to see Eliška in hospital he looked at people in a similar way. Now he was seeing them several times a day. When he asked Kohl about this he explained:

'You are beginning to awaken. The more awakened you are the more you perceive the people around you who are sleeping, and you also instantly become aware of others who are awakening too. They need love and support, just like when a child is being born. You have to look after them, take an interest and be close to them. By the way, do you know what Buddha means? It means nothing more than 'the Awakened One'.'

Tomáš listened with interest. By that time he had got used to sitting on the carpet, which actually struck him as more comfortable than an armchair. He was not restricted by its form, and he could choose any position he wanted. He looked at Kohl and asked, 'Will I ever awaken completely? You know what I mean?'

'I know exactly what you mean. Whatever all the pundits may say about how impossible it is or how it is only achieved once every two thousand years, or how you have to be born that way and so forth, I believe it is possible even for ordinary people. You and I will achieve enlightenment. You might even get there first.'

'But don't you think it requires hours of practice and asceticism?'

'The more you consider that option and try to understand it, the more difficult it is. It's like trying to understand swimming. You won't learn by watching. Ultimately you just have to jump in the water and swim. Did you know that toddlers can swim without being taught?'

'I did. Just as they can be awakened before anybody manages to tell them that they can't.' Both of them burst out laughing here, and Kohl added with tears in his eyes, 'Exactly. You will be a marvellous father, and your child will have an unusual childhood.'

'And what about the rest of his life?'

Kohl understood where he was leading. 'You can give the child everything you have, and provide protection and guidance throughout his childhood, but the way he then chooses is not for you to decide.'

'I know, I know. I only hope I don't disappoint him as a father.'

'You will be an even better father than anything you see in your most wonderful imaginings, Tom.'

'Thank you. In all the time I've known you I've sorted out a heap of problems, including a financial situation that seemed impossible.'

'And how did you manage that?'

'I simply stopped wasting money on stupid things, and I only pay for what I absolutely need.'

When he went home that day he realized how fortunate he was. He had a wonderful wife, a child on the way, marvellous friends like Kohl and Honza, he was healthy, he had work and a nice place to live. What made him happiest at this time was that his life finally had meaning. He felt great, because he knew he had something that others do not have. Everyone has a gift and he had found his. He was proud of how much he helped others by simply being. Every time he helped someone to understand some trivial detail or to sort something out, and he saw the spark in their eyes, he felt fulfilled. Like today in school when he was speaking about love.

More and more friends and acquaintances came to him for advice. They had noticed how balanced he was now, so they wanted to c him over various things, from absolute banalities to highly important matters. Above all, he tried to advise them from his heart, but he soon understood that when he was dealing with somebody's problems then it was his problem too, and they had to sort it out together. He might have looked like he had become a completely different person, but he knew that inside he was still 'good old Tomáš', except that he was no longer afraid to do things the way he felt.

He had worked out that the meaning of life was not to get rid of suffering, but to accept it. To accept it and dance. And to rejoice! To become something more: to make the world a little better than it was yesterday, to illuminate the darkness, to achieve perfection in something and to share it with others. He was dancing inside and his soul was humming away: This is *the life that we all have to live here.*

— • —

Tomáš had liked the last lesson a lot, and he was very much looking forward to the next one. He was always absorbed in thought after a trip to see Kohl. Sometimes they just chatted together, seemingly about nothing in particular. When he thought about it later he realized that their chat about various trivialities and unimportant matters had helped him to understand so many things – and to join them up. Like when you put in place the last piece of a wonderful jigsaw puzzle picture.

Kohl was a great teacher, even if he spoke rather crudely and smoked grass. While not exactly looking the part, he was the most worldly-wise person that Tomáš had ever met. Even though he did not look like the perfect mentor, for Tomáš he was. He looked up to and admired him. Maybe that's how my pupils look at me, he flattered himself. He had tried to think positively of himself ever since Kohl had initiated him in the issues surrounding self-confidence:

'You react to stimuli that are on the same frequency as you are. That is how you become a bad, an average or a good teacher, father, husband and so forth. And that's the way it is with everything.' He hadn't understood very well, so he asked for an example.

'Imagine that three people tell you independently of each other that a) you are an excellent teacher, b) you are an average teacher and

c) you are a bad teacher. What are you going to believe?'

'Whatever I happen to think myself, and that in turn depends on my frequency.'

'Exactly. Now you realize that people do not have to actually say anything. All it takes is the way that those around you think of you and look at you. They are constantly sending out various impulses to you and it's on the basis of your frequency that you choose those you are going to react to.'

'Amazing!'

'So it all starts with you. It all depends on what you think of yourself and the kind of people you are mixing with. People cannot send you impulses with a higher frequency than they already have themselves. That's why you feel so good with people who have a higher energy level than you.'

That might have been why he had recently been surprised when Kohl reproached him, because life is not just about meeting aware people. He had continually failed to understand that lesson. Of course, this did not mean that he had to behave so disrespectfully towards him: I must apologize to him again today, he lamented.

Absorbed in thought, he found the journey passed unusually quickly. He nimbly climbed the stairs to Kohl's office, and opening the door he was surprised to find a young lady working at the table with her back turned towards him. She noticed him before he managed to say anything:

'Oh, you must be Tomáš. Dad often spoke about you. I am Anna.'

'Kohl never mentioned you. I didn't know he has a daughter. Where is he?'

'Ah, Dad was always secretive. He isn't with us any more. He died early yesterday morning,' and she sadly cast down her eyes.

'What?' he managed. 'When? How?'

'He had cancer. He never told you about that, did he? That's why he smoked so much marijuana. It alleviated the pain. He was on a visit to us. I went to wake him up in the morning and, and...' she burst out crying. 'He was beyond help.'

Tomáš was quite beside himself, drained of all energy. His legs shook and he was barely able to speak:

'I didn't even manage to say good-bye,' he stammered. 'When is the funeral?'

Anna wiped her eyes:

'He didn't want us to arrange a funeral. We're just cremating his body and scattering the ashes at his favourite spot in the forest.'

Tomáš pulled himself together a little: 'I am so sorry, Anna. Please accept my sincere condolences.'

'We knew it was coming. He was the best dad in the world,' and with these words she broke down crying again. 'You don't know how it helped him to meet you. He had been getting more and more embittered...' Anna took a deep breath to continue: 'until he met you. He was always talking about you. You gave him hope and something for him to look forward to every day. He liked you a lot. I think he was just waiting until he could pass on everything he knew to you.'

Tomáš could not even recollect how he got home. He was in such awful pain. Nothing could alleviate it. The feeling seemed to tear him to pieces. He could not accept that his friend was gone. He was upset at the entire world and at himself for not saying good-bye. He didn't even get to apologize to him.

The world is so unfair. It wasn't even his time yet. And why did I tell him off so much for smoking? Why didn't he confide in me that he was easing the pain that way? He wondered, as the anger seeped like frost through his entire body.

Why do people like him have to die, when all kinds of bastards live to be a hundred? Why did he have to die? Why him and not me? He asked his soul what it was all supposed to mean, but his soul remained silent. He could not remember what happened next, but he woke up with the same awful feeling he had gone to sleep with.

In the morning he phoned the school to apologize for not coming in because of a family bereavement. He spent the entire day in gloomy thought. Clearly, the growth he had been through was over. Without Kohl he would go back to his old ways, hating himself and the world around him. How he missed him! It had never occurred to him that he might die. He tried to do something about his depression, but he could not even ease it a little.

Eliška stood by him the entire time. She knew how much Kohl had meant for him. She tried to console him as much as possible, looking after him the entire morning. She cooked his meals – otherwise he would not have eaten anything – and she prepared everything he needed to take part in the ceremony. She tried to talk to him, but didn't get very far, so she didn't push him any further. After driving for about an hour they got to the location where the ceremony was due to take place. There were just a few people there. Family and close friends only, apparently. Tomáš got to see Matěj again after all that time.

On that day, which he would never forget, the weather was beautiful. The wind played with the tree branches and dry leaves rustled underfoot. The sun was warming and it was very pleasant in the forest.

Each person spoke briefly from the heart, until it was his and Eliška's turn. She apologized that she had not known Kohl very much and that she was there accompanying Tomáš. He just said a few words:

'When I got to know Kohl I was a self-absorbed, frustrated, unhappy person. Today I am saying good-bye to him as a balanced and loving person. He kindled a light in me, and it is mostly thanks to him that I still carry it in me. It is not to my teacher that I now say good-bye. I shall never forget you, my friend and brother.' When he had finished speaking he wiped the tears from his face and went back to stand next to his wife.

After these speeches, Anna spoke or rather chanted an Native American prayer, thanking Kohl's soul for being what it was and wishing it all the best in its new life. She quietly scattered the ash and began to bid farewell to all. When she came to them she took them both by the hand:

'Your child will be the happiest in the world. You are wonderful people. Tomáš, carry on doing what you started with my father. His soul will be looking over you all the time and will always be close to you.' They thanked her and set off for home.

As they were leaving, Matěj called out: 'Tom.'

'Sorry, I forgot to say goodbye,' and he went over and embraced him. Neither of them needed to say anything, as they both felt the same way. They had lost somebody who was one of the few to understand them. Before he returned to his car, Matěj called out something that Tomáš would never forget:

'Part of him will remain within us for ever!'

He felt rather better than he had the day before. He continually repeated the word love, just as Kohl had taught him, to dispel depression. This barely helped at all, but still made things a little better. His thoughts were slightly calmer when at length his soul spoke to him:

Life is too short. Don't wait for anything; just submerge yourself in it. Seek beauty in everything. Rejoice in the little things and let the large things go. In yourself and in others. He burst out crying like a baby for the first time in a long time.

He remembered the worst things he had ever done: The time he had told his mum he hated her; the time he had tripped up his best friend; the time he was angry at Eliška because they could not have a child, instead of comforting her. Then he remembered the times he had been happiest: At Christmastime when his parents had given him the remote-control car that he had wanted; when he asked for Eliška's hand, and she had answered him: 'Hold on a minute, I'll just check my diary to see if I can fit you in for the rest of my life. Yes!' And then when he spoke to Matěj. He felt so small and insignificant and yet so grand and marvellous. He felt his connection with the whole wide world, just like when spring can be scented in the air after a long hard winter. He felt whole again, and went to sleep with a sense of heavenly bliss and enormous sadness.

— • —

As the days and weeks went by following Kohl's death, he tried to come to terms with it, but with little success. He felt the wound in his heart, a wound that slowly turned into a scar. Without actually knowing why, he called Ondra to see if he would go out for a beer with him. They had not got on very well of late, but he needed someone to talk with now, and it surprised him just how much they did get on. Amongst other things Ondra said:

'You must have liked him a lot. I am sorry about that.'

As he was going back home the snow beneath his feet crunched pleasantly. At last he had understood that lesson. Things had been really excellent today with Ondra. It no longer bothered him what level his friend was on. Quite the reverse. He realized he wasn't perfect, but he wasn't playing at anything and he was his own man. Authentic. Everybody is better in some way, and more unique, than others. He told himself off: I was stupid when I thought he had nothing to give me! And who can judge how far anybody is at all?

He felt a slight movement in his soul and recognized Kohl's presence. He looked up at the starry sky and whispered: 'Thank you, my friend.'

Part two: We

2/12 The connector

Tomáš leant back on the hard bench and stretched out his legs. One expectant mother after another was sitting in the waiting room. Their bellies were often so large that he wondered what he would do if the first one started giving birth. Fortunately, Eliška's examination came to an end before that happened. Several months had passed since Kohl's death. The feeling of emptiness had slowly subsided, but he presumed it would never go away completely. What he had feared so much had not actually happened. It seemed his energy level had not fallen significantly. He still felt considerably better off than before he had met Kohl. The closer the due date came, the more often he wondered whether or not he would make a good father. Eliška was already a responsible mother. She paid enormous attention to her diet and studied various literature on pregnancy and parenting. The baby was due in a month.

After considering his strengths and weaknesses for some time he
recalled what Kohl had once told him:

'It all starts with you. If you think you're going to be a good father,
then you will be.'

'I do miss you, my friend,' he sighed.

— • —

Tomáš had started to take an interest of late in current affairs. He had
noticed the growing tension in society, followed the increasing number of local conflicts on television and it did not leave him with a very
good feeling. It had never affected him this badly.

Now he was watching the foreign news more and more: various
discussions on the economic crisis and the frequent demonstrations
of unemployed youth all over the world. He tried to understand it all.

He felt that something was missing in his life. He did not know
what it was or when he had lost it. It occurred to him that he should
try to find some like-minded people online – people who were trying to give their lives meaning. This decision cheered him up, as he
felt his soul moving gently within him.

He tried discussions and websites on philosophy and the soul, but
they were usually all cranks, and on one occasion he even came up
against a practitioner of black magic! He did not get on very well, and
they never saw each other again. Tomáš was rather afraid he might
use some dark practices on him, but then he reassured himself that
he had not given him any reason to do so.

Social networks were not really for him, because they seemed so
impersonal. On the other hand he could get to know people there who
were themselves seeking. One day he was contacted by a young woman. She was a member of the same group that he was in (discussing
sociology and the soul). She wrote him a short message:

'Are you Tomáš Jedlička?'

'Yes, just as it says in my profile,' he looked heavenwards as he wrote back.

She then started asking him for the city where he lived, his profession and the like. Marvellous. Some adolescent wants to chat me up, he started thinking. Some time later he answered her questions and showed no further interest in her, until she sent the following message:

'I was supposed to find you. I am Naďa, the connector. You are to meet up with your team. Apologies for the inquisitive questions, but I had to be sure it was you.'

All of a sudden he sat up in his chair and came to attention.

'What? What do you mean?'

'Just as I wrote. I am able to feel certain things. I have the ability to bring together groups of people who are meant to know each other. Thanks to me they get to meet much sooner. You are to meet five people. The first is a businessman, the second a programmer, the third a writer, the fourth a pure light and the fifth a former policewoman. The meeting is planned for Thursday next week at three in the afternoon.'

Tomáš was totally astounded by the woman's self-assurance. When he read the first few sentences he thought it was some stupid joke, but after a while he started to take it rather more seriously.

'And what are we supposed to meet for?'

'I will tell you at the meeting. I will tell you everything I know.'

'How do you find different people, and how do you know they belong together? How can I know you are telling me the truth?'

'I have highly developed intuition. I communicate with higher intelligences through visions and images. I am gradually putting together a mosaic and trying to find all the members of the team and to contact them. It used to be a lot more difficult in the past. Now we have social networks and people are more interconnected, it is easier. I have been looking for you six for over a year. I actually had the biggest problem finding you. You could be seen in a very pure light, but then you disappeared from me for a couple of months.'

He did not understand why, but his confidence in her increased with every mail, even though it seemed incredible to him that he was going along like that with a girl he had never met before, who could basically have been anybody.

After an hour-long conversation she asked him:

'Can I count on your attendance? It is very important that you come.'

'I will definitely come,' he wrote back, as it flashed through his mind: I'd never have guessed I would ever do this. Naďa thanked him for trusting her and only then wrote the exact address for the meeting place. She then immediately finished the conversation.

It was as if something that had died along with Kohl had now reawoken within him. He began to feel his soul more again. Only now did he realize that it had hardly spoken to him for the last half year. He had not given it space for all of six months, as if it didn't exist at all. Throughout this time he had actually had little energy, though he did not fully realize it until now. He remembered that he had not been behaving all that well towards people of late. He had forgotten a lot of the things that Kohl had taught him, but above all he had forgotten to use his heart. His soul whispered: *All this time I have spoken to you, but you have not listened.* His eyes misted over and a pleasant warm sensation came over him.

2/13 The hooded boy

Tomáš was aching and tired all over. He had not slept a wink all night, or if he had managed to for a while, the cold soon woke him up. He was shaking all over. It was dark in the dormitory and the grave-like silence was occasionally interrupted by somebody's snoring, as another fifty men slept there too. He remembered where he was and what was happening up above. They were barely surviving like rats underground as their entire world had shrunk down to this basement shelter. They couldn't trust one other. Chaos and despair were everywhere. Some rather sophisticated modern-day concentration camps, called adaptation centres by their creators, had been established all over the world. They had not managed to agree on which group of people to blame, so the inmates were of various backgrounds and faiths. Humanity had not learnt from its past. When people lose all their security, they start to believe any old lies, so things had got so out of hand that innocent people were being killed, women and children included. And even before all this I used to think the world was unfair, he thought as he slowly sat up.

This kind of thing was best done by dogmatic leaders. All over the world dozens of them had got into power, sometimes based on religion and other times on race, a particular nation, communism, neocapitalism or other ideologies. They often highlighted the arrival of a New Age, with a new order to be created, and they sacrificed themselves to achieve this. But all these so-called leaders had one thing in common. They had seized power without much ado, tortured all their opponents and sent them to adaptation centres or simply murdered them. Some people in the shelter said there was nothing to fear up above. They said it was all an expedient lie, propaganda, to keep them down there and under control.

Tomáš's feet touched the cold, dirty floor. The men and women there often called it the 'final war', usually meaning that it would destroy all humanity. A couple of the crazies insisted that if they survived they would steer well clear of war in future, but that humanity deserved nothing more than to fry in hell.

'At last God has punished us for our sins! It was wrong to provoke him with our debauched lifestyle, and clearly he has now determined the time we shall all perish,' they preached.

Like most people in the shelter, he doubted that things would ever turn out right. He knew the world would never again be the way it used to be. Not after all that had happened. It was only momentum that kept him going.

At last the first lights came on. The electricity in the shelter only worked a little, and it often failed. Drinking water was rationed, along with food and clothing. He had to watch out for the chip inserted in his arm, which authorized him to eat and drink every day. The local crooks would not have hesitated to kill him for it. When people are dying of hunger they are capable of anything.

The others would get up soon. He took a bite out of a leftover dry roll from out of his trouser pocket and headed off for the sick bay. His skin had recently been very pale, and his arms were covered in a strange, itchy rash. He hoped the nurse would be able to advise him. Only a couple of lights worked in the corridor, while the other bulbs flickered from time to time, creating a very gloomy atmosphere. Flicker. The air reeked of burning plastic, stinging his eyes. Flicker, flicker. The sick bay was about a twenty-minute walk away through the south tunnel, but eventually he had to choose another route, because during the night there had been a cave-in. A group of police-supervised zeros were clearing up the rubble.

It was not difficult to identify the zeros. They had a large zero sewn onto their right shoulder, meaning they were of no importance to the shelter inhabitants, so they did not receive rations or a place to sleep. Tomáš knew that as soon as the number of children at the school dropped below a certain level then he or one of his colleagues would also receive this designation. Zeros were used for the worst work that nobody else wanted to do. As soon as you were given that patch you never got rid of it.

As he drew closer to his destination the stench grew worse, as he slowly realized that it was not plastic that was burning, but human remains. For practical reasons the mortuary was close to the sick bay. The shelter inhabitants were plagued by numerous diseases, which meant a short trip to the mortuary. Fortunately, this is just a little thing I've got, he thought as he walked through the door.

'What do you need, teacher?' a repulsive old nurse shouted. He had a letter K sewn onto his shoulder, which indicated the Metro station that was used as a school. That way everybody could tell who he was.

'I've got this weird rash, and I don't know what to do with it,' he said as he rolled up his sleeve.

'First fill out Form 147,' she said, pointing to it on the table.

He glanced over it and signed. It said that if the sick bay staff considered him a risk to the others in the shelter they could give him a lethal injection without his knowledge. Then the nurse put on her rubber gloves and examined his forearm for the moment.

'Scabies. It's been rife round here lately. I'll prescribe you this ointment. You'll probably catch it again in a couple of weeks, but this'll help you for now.'

He did not say anything, but just sadly bowed his head. That is all I need, he thought.

'Now off you go. I want to catch up on my rest, before they bring some more of the dying. There were several cave-ins yesterday. I don't have time for people like you.'

He was going to thank her, but then he realized that he would just be needlessly drawing attention to himself. He looked at his scuffed old watch and realized he only had fifteen minutes to get to school. He set out through the west tunnel. It was the fastest way there, even though it was not the most suitable. It had been partly flooded and led through the local 'poor quarter', inhabited mostly by sick people who could no longer do their work. They were subsequently designated as zeros and the local society kept them just in case. There was no water or clean air and they usually only survived a couple of weeks. Flicker. Flicker.

No matter how hard he tried to suppress them, memories resurfaced of the day the first bomb fell. He was with Eliška in a shopping centre when the sirens went off. Panic ensued. Everybody wanted to get to the safety of the underground garages. He grabbed her by the hand and they ran towards the stairs together. On the way he saw a wrinkled old woman in a red dress. She hadn't noticed the confusion all around her and carried on quietly shopping. He shouted at her to take cover, but she did not react. They got to the garage in time. Their car had been smashed in at the front, but otherwise it was all right. They sat there and waited. Flicker. It lasted about an hour. The longest, most awful sixty minutes of their lives. He presumed that the nuclear bomb had been dropped by Russia, which was on the verge of war with Europe.

This was followed by an announcement on the radio. The bomb had fallen on another city. The Governor said there was no danger of another attack. At least in the next few hours. At that time they did not consider that tens of thousands of innocent people had died and that this was just the beginning. They were glad that death had passed them by this time. Until they found out it had fallen on Prague.

His thoughts were interrupted by some kind of noise, and amongst other things his shoes were getting damp inside. The noise was coming from somewhere behind him. He turned round and saw three shadows on the tunnel walls. Flicker, flicker. He began to make out the silhouettes of running figures, and recognized from their reflective bands that two of them were local police. The third, whom they were pursuing, quickly drew up close to him. He was of fairly small stature and held something in his hand, which could have been a weapon. Tomáš's entire body was immobilized by fear.

He stood stock still and watched the scene unfold. The closer the three of them got to him, the louder was the threatening sound of splashing water. The men got so close that he could tell what they were shouting. His heart was pounding somewhere up in his throat, as they yelled:

'Stop, or I'll fire.'

The fugitive was only a few steps away. He was a child with a hood on. The shots rang out all over the tunnels, ricocheting several times as echoes. Now his right ear could not hear anything, while there was a tremendous whistling in his left ear. Horrified, he moved towards the falling figure. A boy of some ten years of age lay in the dirty water, shaking with cold. He was in shock, as he clutched a loaf and stared off into emptiness somewhere. Tomáš watched the dying child and felt so ill that he had to bend down and throw up. The water splashed several times as digested pieces of bread roll fell into it.

He raised his head. Flicker. He stopped breathing in fright. Two burly policemen stood about ten metres from him. They pointed their guns and one of them shouted:

'Who are you?'

It was at this moment that he woke up perspiring. His heart was pounding so much, he had the feeling it was about to leap out of his chest. Eliška was sleeping quietly beside him. It was just a dream, thank God! he sighed inwardly in relief. But not for long.

What had appeared in previous dreams to be a horror film set sometime in the distant future was not so remote now. It was actually carrying on quite seamlessly from what was going on in the world today. For some time he felt himself drowning in the whirlpool of these darkest thoughts. Then he raised his energy level as Kohl had taught him and fell back to sleep.

2/14 The team

Eliška noticed that Tomáš had recently been feeling down. He wasn't eating much, and what was more, his face had lost the expression of happiness and a life lived to the full, which had been so typical of him.

'What's the matter, dear?' she asked him over supper.

'The dreams have come back. Now they're even worse than they were,' and he carried on eating. She moved over to him, stroked his back and fell silent.

As Thursday drew closer he felt increasingly insecure about the meeting agreed online. He was not the type to believe in such things. If he had not formed the habit of not changing his mind when he lacked energy he would not have gone. On the Wednesday evening he repleted his energy with a brief meditation. For a while he lost his sense of insecurity and even felt a gentle urge to take part in the meeting. He wanted to get to know these people. Something drew him to them, which also struck him as ridiculous, considering he did not actually know them.

After school he set off for the city centre, where the meeting was to take place. He was walking down a busy street, when he was again beset by doubts: I've been taken in by some adolescent online. What a fool I am. I've been as naive as a little kid. She is definitely not all there. Or she's having a good laugh about how gullible I am!

He arrived a little later than he'd expected to, but fortunately it was still a few minutes before three. Following his instructions he took the lift up to the seventh floor and rang at No. 53. A young lady whom he immediately recognized answered the door. It was Naďa, just as she looked in her online photo. Her low neckline struck him immediately. She looked much better in the flesh. She smiled at him, showing her marvellous white teeth, turned round and called, 'We're all here now!'

The apartment looked pleasant and had a nice fragrance. There were some ten pairs of shoes in the hallway. Tomáš took his off, noticed a large black-framed mirror and proceeded into the spacious living room, centring round a dark wooden table, on which there was a jug of water and a sign: Help yourself! Several people were sitting around the table in chairs and armchairs. Tomáš did not feel all that good among so many strangers.

Before he managed to say anything, Naďa took the floor.

'For a long time I have been working towards this meeting today. You have an important task in front of you. You are the strongest group that I have ever put together. The world is collapsing. I feel it in my bones. When you set aside all your prejudices, you will feel it too. Your paths needed to be brought together a little earlier, so you could intercede... Dimitri is at the head of the table as the father of the group. Next to him is Kristýna, who is to be its mother. She has great powers of empathy. Dimitri knows everything that can be known about this world – nothing has remained concealed from him. Jirka is the one in the blue armchair. He is the manager of a marketing company. He knows people's minds and has great powers of persuasion. Marek is the computer expert. He has the capacity to obtain important information, while also being able to put it together perfectly. He knows how the world today is interconnected, so he understands the ultimate effects if any of his key nodes fail. Tomáš, who has just arrived, is a teacher. He has overcome several limitations that he has confronted. He can also do that with other people – he is your catalyst.' At this he felt a pleasant warmth in his back.

Naďa looked each one of them in the eye in turn:

'Our last team member is Karla, but she could not be with us today, as she is in prison. Her position in the team has not yet been revealed to me. Your roles are not firmly established either. Nothing is fixed. What I said was true a minute ago, but it may be different now. My task is at an end. Thank you for coming, and I wish you all the best.'

Her eyes shone as she spoke these words. She clearly meant them with absolute sincerity. Tomáš was now glad that he had come.

Dimitri, a charismatic, elderly man with a full beard asked:

'Naďa, what is our task?'

'You have to stop him. I don't know his name, but I know he is very dangerous. He does not see and he does not hear. He is driving us into a place from which there is no escape.'

A likeable middle-aged man with a familiar, smoothly shaven

face and a tailor-made suit, whose name Tomáš had forgotten, asked a question which had occurred to him too:

'How do we find him?'

'He's a man who has played a significant role in Karla's life. So we have to contact her as soon as possible. I have given Dimitri the information required to get to her. Now I must leave you.'

She put on a brown suede coat and smiled for the last time as she left.

The silence that usually falls very quickly over a room full of mutual strangers was not disturbed until Dimitri spoke up:

'Well, I am just as confused as you are. I, too, would like to know why we are all here.'

Kristýna was the first to answer. She looked around thirty, with a nice little nose, while her comely face seemed to be constantly smiling:

'Like Naďa I feel this is an important task. This is not the last time we shall see each other.'

Immediately remarkable for his unusually gaunt figure, unshaven face and tousled hair, Marek raised his voice:

'Does it not strike you as weird at all just how we have got here? What information must she have on us all? I don't intend to say anything, until somebody tells me what's going on!'

Dimitri wanted to respond, but Kristýna gestured for him not to:

'Marek, your doubts are well-founded. Without you we could easily be taken in by somebody. Now please listen to your intuition. I know you listen to it occasionally – otherwise you wouldn't be here. What is it telling you?'

'It's telling me to sit down here and shut up, until I have something constructive to say.'

Tomáš felt like bursting out laughing, but he held back. He did not want to draw attention to himself unnecessarily.

The man in the suit took the floor. 'So to summarize, by some strange coincidence we have all gathered here today. It has something to do with the world situation. I don't know how much you are interested in current affairs, so I will tell you what I basically know.'

'Thank you, Jirka,' said Kristýna. 'Please carry on.'

He spoke in a pleasant, engaging manner that made it evident he had broad experience of public speaking. 'The entire problem stems from the current structure of the system. The banks are simply too big to be allowed to go bankrupt. The system is so interconnected that if one falls then they all fall. The same goes for state structures. If one of the Western states falls then the others will soon follow suit. This results in uncertainty on the markets, high unemployment and inflation.'

Dimitri was pensively stroking his dark grey beard. 'This gives rise to people's increasing frustration and their fears for the future.'

Even though he was a successful entrepreneur, Jirka was very well aware of ordinary people's situations. 'It used to be true that when people worked hard they could afford a house, a car and education for their children. This has long ceased to be the case these days. Paradoxically, people graft like mad and still don't get anywhere in life. Or they take out a loan to study at college, and then they can't find work.'

Dimitri added: 'They're shouting in the squares and grumbling in the pubs. 'Let's have some security at long last. We have nothing left to fall back on.' World political leaders have succumbed to fear. They have become so afraid of the situation that has arisen that they would rather save the banks that should have gone under, thus merely postponing and aggravating developments that have to run their course in any case.'

Marek hit the nail on the head. 'Thus showing the people who were behind the crisis just how much society is dependent on them. That they can basically do whatever they please, and we are going to put up with it.'

'That was a decision based on fear,' Kristýna said. 'If you love someone that does not mean you allow them to do anything.'

'You're right,' Dimitri said. 'The old system and the people at the top are afraid of losing power, so they do whatever it takes to protect it.'

'Which is not bad,' Kristýna said. 'Political leaders, bankers and representatives of the old system are just doing what they're best able to do. They can't imagine any other world. They're so absorbed in the present-day system that they don't see any other options apart from doing everything possible to preserve the current status quo at any price.'

Kristýna spoke very wisely, which gave Tomáš the courage to finally speak up. 'You're quite right. I understand they don't mean any harm, but their actions are only provoking unrest. Tensions are rising all over the world. What's more, it's not just a matter of who has more power or money. People are getting more and more unhappy about all the dishonesty, corruption, increasing aggression and indifference.'

'People feel that if it wasn't for them, the politicians and bankers wouldn't be there,' said Marek. 'Ordinary people get the impression that the top leaders in the current system are hardly bending over backwards to help them.'

Kristýna wasn't happy that the discussion had taken this turn. 'It isn't right to speak about them as people separate from the rest of humanity. They're people just like us. They have families and children. They aren't happy about what's going on in the world either. They're overwhelmed by fear, just like everybody else is. But do carry on, Marek.'

Tomáš was very impressed by the way she spoke. She was compassionate, and yet she was not afraid to speak the truth. He added, 'Kristýna is right. People have stopped listening to one other. They think they're separate from each other. They should listen to their souls more.'

Dimitri understood immediately what he was talking about. 'What you are talking about now, Tom, is called the theory of separation and the theory of union. People are interconnected. Everybody else is basically our second self. We shouldn't perceive them as outside ourselves. Of course, it has worked this way for the last few hundred years, which was also the reason for all the wars and conflicts. I believe it will all soon change, because more and more people are becoming aware of the union. Our aim is to create a better system, a system to reflect the development of human society. Over the last hundred years, people have undergone tremendous development, but the system is still just as outdated. Parliamentarianism developed in the 19th century, before the internet and other modern media.'

'Before people had awoken and become interconnected. Notice that most movements are non-violent. People appreciate human life a lot more,' Kristýna said.

Tomáš wanted to mention his dreams. From what he remembered of them, the future of humanity was not going to be so non-violent. Still, he preferred not to say anything – he did not yet trust his new acquaintances enough. I wouldn't want to alarm them unnecessarily, he thought.

Marek had a mouth full of biscuits, so he could barely be understood:

'Well, it'th all very nice what you're talking about here, but let'th get back down to earth. Why are we here today? I know there'th some great global transformation in store for us, but what have we got to do with all that?' and his crumbs fell all over.

'I like the way you're so down-to-earth, Marek,' said Kristýna. 'I think our first task is to contact Karla. That way we can find out who this unknown man is that we're meant to stop.'

Marek snorted and put his empty plate on the table. 'When Naďa first contacted me I thought you'd just be a bunch of headcases. After our discussion today I have to admit that you do have a good overview of things, even if you are a bit up in the clouds there. You have your own opinions and you're different to other people. You don't behave like sheep. I'll help you. I'll get some info on Karla for you.'

Dimitri looked around the other members of this newly formed and at first sight highly heterogeneous team:

'It's time to end the meeting. Let's think it all over. Do not let anyone know what we have been talking about. We shall have our next meeting here on Monday at 5 pm.'

'Come if you want to,' Kristýna added.

When Tomáš stepped out into the street it was already dark and considerably colder than it had been. He stepped up his pace a little just to warm up. On the one hand he was enthusiastic to have met people like that. They all made an impression on him, and Dimitri had great charisma. Kristýna had an extremely high energy level, and Jirka was very pleasant and cheerful. Neither money nor success had spoiled him. Then again Marek was sincere, and spoke as he found. Tomáš also felt slightly apprehensive that this might all be some kind of hoax. And then for a while he wondered if it had not been a mistake on his part to avoid speaking about his dreams. He justified his hesitation to himself like this: Not even my wife knows exactly what my dreams are about. Why should I tell others?

— • —

Pregnancy looked good on Eliška. She had also recently been looking after herself a lot – she got plenty of sleep, kept to a healthy diet, stopped drinking alcohol entirely and often watched comedies and films with a positive message. He very much appreciated her responsible attitude towards pregnancy. On a couple of occasions he had caught her crying at the television, but these weren't the tears he had been used to with her. Now they were really gushing and the paper handkerchiefs were lying all around. Sometimes he watched alongside her. The films were too saccharine sweet for his taste, but he liked to sit beside her with his hand placed on her stomach. The baby was kicking more and more often now.

— • —

This time Tomáš arrived at the No. 53 apartment meeting well in advance. They still had to wait for Marek. Meantime he got talking with Jirka, confiding that their baby was due in two weeks' time. Jirka was really enthusiastic about this – his sober expression was suddenly out of the window. He described how on edge he had been when Metoděj, his elder son, was born. Now he was three years old. Then they chatted about correct upbringing. Jirka had quite clear views on this. 'Competition and games – not everything in life should be for free. That's what I teach my children from an early age. Of course, they don't have to compete for their parents' love.'

Tomáš basically agreed, and the conversation presently moved on to Jirka's work: 'So you're the man behind Best Systems?! I heard that you won an award for best marketing. Ah, so now I know why you're so familiar. I've seen you on TV,' and he could barely hide his astonishment.

'Right, that's me. I don't like to talk about it. When I tell people, they want to borrow money off me straight away!' Jirka joked. His sense of humour was definitely up Tomáš's street.

Kristýna made some excellent tea and was now putting some freshly baked biscuits on the table. 'When I first saw Apartment No. 53 I was stunned by just how perfect it was. Lots of space, everything just right and in its right place. I had to work on it to get at least a little warmth and love into it, so we felt at home here. Bon appetit.'

Marek appeared in the doorway, limping like an old man. He immediately found himself complaining. 'Apologies for being late. I fell on the stairs at home. Bloody hell. You know how in the films the dog runs to see if his master is okay? Well, my little blighter just sat there on the sofa and ignored me.' The entire episode amused everybody. Then he added, 'Here's the info on Karla. I think you'll be very surprised. It wasn't difficult to find something on her. At one time she was being written about a lot in the newspapers.'

Dimitri nodded. 'Marek's right. I've found out quite a bit about her myself. Not that I wouldn't have believed you, Marek, but I like my information to be from more than one source. Do please carry on.'

Marek grimaced. 'It's kind of a well-worn story. When Karla was out on her beat one night, she and her partner were called out to a suspected burglary. When they arrived they saw a guy running away from the scene. After that their testimonies vary.'

'In what way?' Jirka asked.

'I'm just getting to that. Her partner, name of Musílek, says that Karla shot and killed the unarmed burglar on the spot.' Silence descended on the room.

Dimitri looked fully into Tomáš's incredulous face.

'That's true. Karla's now doing five years in prison for manslaughter.'

'At first, I thought it was a clear-cut case too. An exhausted policewoman had simply made a mistake. Sure, it was just her word against his, but then Musílek was respected by the police. Then they promoted him immediately, and several times more after that. Now he is Deputy Police Commissioner. Nobody believed Karla's testimony, which was rather full of holes.'

'How do you mean?' Kristýna asked.

'She said Musílek killed the burglar. When he realized he didn't have a weapon on him, he supposedly leaned on her to state in her report that she saw a pistol on him, and he promised to take care of the rest himself. She refused and ended up behind bars. Her partner's case was helped by the fact that the weapon used to shoot the burglar belonged to Karla.'

Hands behind his head, Jirka sat down in his armchair looking very pensive. 'And what about fingerprints and other evidence?'

'I found out everything I could about the case, but it's not clear whether or not she was the one who killed the burglar. The least that can be said is that the entire case really stinks.'

Dimitri praised Marek. 'I see you are really true to your reputation. You found out plenty, including the kind of info that an ordinary person wouldn't get hold of!' So for the rest of the evening Marek wore a rather smug smile. He would have floated up to the ceiling with pride if he could.

Jirka was still pensive. 'How many years does she have till the end of her prison sentence?'

'I thought nobody was going to ask. I've found out all that too. I'm your man when it comes to information,' and he puffed up so much, it was a wonder he did not burst.

Jirka knew this kind of whizz kid. Several of them worked for him. For the time being, he decided not to prick his bloated ego with a pin. 'Well, you definitely have no lack of self-confidence.'

'You bet, Jirka. They're holding Karla at Mírov Prison, in a special section there for the police. She wouldn't last long among the other criminals. She's almost served two years of her sentence. To cut a long story short: it's too early for her to be released for good behaviour.'

'We could try to introduce some new facts to the case,' said Kristýna.

'It's a good idea,' said Dimitri, 'but it would take too long. I don't think we have that much time.'

'What do you suggest?' asked Jirka.

Kristýna's eyes flashed: 'Let's drive out there and take a look. It will have to be this Thursday. I feel it.'

'Well, I'm sure it's crazy,' said Marek, 'but I'm in.' Dimitri joined them. Kristýna looked at Tomáš sympathetically: 'You should come too. You're our catalyst and I feel you'll be needed there.'

Tomáš resisted: 'What are you going to need me of all people for?'

'Oh, please,' she smiled at him with her transparent blue eyes.

'Well, I hope it's going to be worth it!' he eventually said, by way of confirmation.

2/15 In prison

On the Thursday the children were on holiday, so Tomáš did not have to worry his head over what he would say at school. It wasn't so easy with Eliška. When he lied to her with a heavy heart: 'I'm off to the mountains with some friends, dear,' he promised himself that he would not do it again. As it turned out, this white lie achieved its purpose very nicely. On the day she was in a pleasant mood and looking forward to giving birth very soon.

He met up with Dimitri and Marek on the city outskirts. He got in the car and they set off for Mírov, which was about 150 kilometres away. During this time they spoke for the most part about Kohl and what he had meant to Tomáš. Dimitri showed a lot of sympathy.

'You must have liked him a lot.'

'Oh yes, I did. I often think about him. He helped me a lot in my life, or rather what he taught me still helps me.'

Marek was listening to all this, but for some reason did not comment. Over the last few kilometres they passed through thick forest. Some truly marvellous trees were growing there in the foothills. The sturdy trunks with dense foliage reminded him of the landscape around Ondra's chalet.

When they got to the prison complex they parked in the reserved car park for visitors as indicated by a guard. There weren't many spaces. They probably don't get many visitors driving out here, Tomáš thought. Dimitri asked Marek to stay in the car. 'Karla might find too many people intimidating.'

Marek did not look all that keen, but he did not argue. Judging by the architectural style, Tomáš thought the complex was built in the 1950s.

Dimitri repeated: 'I called yesterday to see if we could visit Karla.

I'm writing my latest book about her, and you are assisting me.' Tomáš nodded. When some guards passed them with a dog, he found it quite disconcerting. If the Alsatian had not been on a leash, he might well have run off.

The prison guards led them through winding corridors to the visiting room. An unpleasant feeling had weighed down on him even before they reached the gate, and now it was pressing even harder. The building and its facilities looked well-maintained, but there was an oppressive atmosphere all around that was choking him. He could not bear it when his freedom was being restricted, and now they seemed to be leading him in chains to a cell where he was to spend the rest of his life. He imagined the mocking looks of his adversaries and the tearful faces of those close to him. A shiver ran down his spine and his throat dried up. But this was nothing compared to what was to come.

After walking for a couple of minutes into the depths of the prison he heard shooting nearby.

The guard accompanying them shouted out, 'Wait here! Don't move!' and drawing his revolver, he ran off towards the sound of gunfire. Tomáš had no problem at all obeying this order. Both of his legs had turned to stone and gone quite numb. He felt as if someone had thrust a hand into his stomach and given it a twist.

Dimitri ducked down and drew Tomáš towards him. He must have looked deadly pale, because Dimitri was holding him up to stop him from falling.

'What's going on?' he barely managed to utter.

Dimitri stared fixedly at the door at the end of the corridor. 'I don't know. Perhaps a prisoner has tried to escape.'

To their dismay, a figure appeared in the doorway. Her clothing was definitely not that of a guard. Tomáš was unable to manage a single word. He had never been in a situation like that before, and right now he just wanted to get away. Shots rang out again. The figure at the end of the corridor took fright at the gunfire just as much as Tomáš and Dimitri did.

He brought to mind the total despair that he had felt when he saw the dead child in his dream. He wanted to vomit, but managed to keep his breakfast down in his stomach, which was still being twisted from side to side, as if about to be wrenched out of his body. But clearly this was a reality he was not going to awaken from. The seconds passed by so slowly. The entire world had now dissipated. Nothing existed but that corridor, with them on one side and the stranger on the other.

She ran over to them. As the slim figure with long plaited hair drew near, Dimitri stood up and shouted, 'It's Karla!'

She raised her hand and thumped him in the face, yelling, 'Shut the fuck up! You're going to help me get out of here. Come on, I won't harm you, unless you don't hurry up and I have to give you another one!'

'Have you gone mad, Karla?' Tomáš gasped for breath.

She thumped him too, so the next thing that he remembered was Dimitri supporting him under his arm as all three ran out of the building.

He could barely control his legs. He had no idea where they were going, but they soon got out. Again they heard gunfire. This time it was a series of shots. When they got to the car Marek was horrified. 'What the bloody hell is going on? I almost crapped myself. Who's shooting in there? And what's she doing here? Did you have a gun with you or something?'

Dimitri answered him calmly. 'I don't know what's going on in there. Karla here has taken us hostage. We have to get out of here!'

All around dogs could be heard barking, which totally paralysed Tomáš. And he had thought things couldn't get any worse.

'Are you crazy? Do you want them to lock us all up?'

Before Dimitri could waste any time explaining, Karla landed a model right hook on Marek too, adding:

'So you don't feel left out. Now move it! All of you! Get in and drive.'

When they were in the car she kept goading them on:

'Come on! It's not safe here.'

Tomáš was still totally out of it. It took him three tries to close the door, which now seemed enormously heavy. His brain could only process one piece of information: Get away fast! Get away fast! He could not think of anything else. Karla ordered:

'Right here! There's another gate that isn't guarded so much.'

And if Tomáš thought it could not get any worse then he was wrong. A prison guard stood at the prison gate – just one man, but armed. When he saw them hurtling towards him he reached for his gun.

Marek yelled, 'Fuck! Fuck! Fuck!', but the guard was surprised and clumsy. Before he managed to draw his gun, their car had passed him by. Tomáš turned round and saw him staring after them and talking into his radio. A few hundred metres further on they joined the road they had come in on. After driving on for another minute, Marek stopped biting his lip.

'What the fuck was all that? What is that woman doing here? Does she have a gun?'

Karla wiped the sweat from her brow. Her pale, gaunt face was dominated by two enormous circles under her eyes. Now she answered in a calmer voice.

'No, I don't. And I apologize for punching you, but it wouldn't have worked any other way. You wouldn't have gone along, and in any case it makes things simpler for you. Step on it!' Again her voice grew harsh. 'You're going too slow. That way they'll soon catch us.'

Marek's normal self-assurance returned to him. 'Who the fuck do you think I am? Bleeding Semir from Cobra 11 or something?'

'Take that track across the field,' Karla yelled.

He turned quite sharply and drove into a forest. Tomáš's stomach turned another somersault. Soon they could hear police sirens from the main road, and they stared at each other in trepidation. Tomáš hugely regretted letting himself be cajoled into coming. He breathed in quickly, but still lacked air.

Karla looked round, calmed down a little and then tried to explain. 'I don't know what was actually happening in there. The day before yesterday I noticed a lot of whispering going on among the prisoners, but I didn't consider it important. The guards have been having a hard time managing lately. Today they were taking me off to the visiting room where somebody wanted to meet me about some book. I presume that was you. They sat me down there and then I heard those shots,' and she closed her eyes as if she didn't want to think about it any more. 'One of the guards ran off to see what was going on. Then the prisoners broke into the room and shot the second guard. I could only watch. If I hadn't been wearing prison clothes and handcuffs they would definitely have shot me too, but they just kicked me in the stomach until I fell off my chair,' and she examined her chafed elbows. 'Luckily, I didn't actually faint. I knew I had to get away. I somehow managed to unlock the handcuffs with a key from the dead guard. He wasn't breathing – he was beyond help, so I ran out into the corridor and that's where I met you. Taking you as hostages was the best plan that came to my mind at the time. I knew you'd have a car.'

Dimitri smoothed his beard. 'The prisons have been overcrowded of late. There has been some minor rioting, but nobody expected anything like this, surely.' As he examined their kidnapper his lips curled slightly upwards. 'We are indeed the visitors you were expecting.'

The forest track was quite rugged, and the car jerked around fitfully. Tomáš was really angry. 'And why did you escape? Don't you realize that if they catch you they'll put you away for life somewhere?'

'Oh, thank you, Mr Cleverdick,' said Karla. 'As if I didn't know that.'

They gradually drove deeper into the forest. The potholes got worse, until they were barely moving at a walking pace. Marek tried to avoid the largest holes and remarked:

'How so?'

'I was never meant to get out of that prison,' said Karla. 'That bastard tried it once and next time he would definitely have succeeded. He bribed somebody to hide drugs in my shoes. It was only by chance that I found out a couple of minutes before a check and got rid of them.'

'Which bastard?' asked Dimitri.

'My old partner. The one who put me in there.'

'Musílek? What the...?' Tomáš could not contain his surprise.

'Where do you know him from? Who are you three anyway?'

'That'll be a long story. Right now we have to get back on the motorway as quickly as possible. I think we could hide you somewhere for a couple of days. Put my sweater on to cover up that prison outfit,' Dimitri said.

Tomáš was amazed at just how resourcefully, decisively and clear-mindedly Dimitri was acting. He was definitely not able to act like that. But then at the same time this made him furious. He shouted at Dimitri, 'Have you gone mad? What if they catch us? We'll get put away too. I'm not going along with this!'

Dimitri tried to calm Tomáš down. 'We're still her hostages. Nothing'll happen to us. We'll clear everything up at Kristýna's. It'll be okay, Tom. Marek, can you find your way to the motorway?'

'I think so. Hopefully there won't be any barriers anywhere. Dimitri's right. Even if they caught us now, we're still her hostages, so we'd be in no danger. Policewoman Plod here has got it sussed. I suggest we get rid of my car as soon as possible, that is, not get rid of it completely.' He tapped on the strip flooring and muttered, 'don't worry, honey'. Then aloud: 'Then the police will return it to me, but we can't stay in it now!'

'I can't believe you want to go along with all this, Marek,' Tomáš snapped as he put his hands in his armpits and decided not to say any more. If his soul had not soothed him he would have jumped out of the slowly moving car straight away. He was frightened to death, as the gunshots kept ringing out in his head and he could vividly imagine the dead guard with his blue shirt slowly absorbing the red blood as his body went cold. What if it had been him instead? Would the police have rung on his doorbell? Mrs Jedlíčka? It's about your husband. Eliška would obviously never have believed them. After all, he would never have lied to her about visiting a prison! Then she would have collapsed in tears – the police would have tried to catch her – their shouts resounding all over the block – the neighbours peeping out from their flats – trying to see what was going on. Why? Why did he go there? 'Why didn't he say anything to me? God, what am I going to do now?' as she clings to her rounded stomach.

The forest thinned out, and the sun again started to shine through the tree branches. Soon a main road appeared, which they cautiously joined. The signposts said it was eight kilometres to the motorway. Their nervousness increased, but then dissipated as they drove onto it and were absorbed in the dense traffic.

Dimitri reached into his pocket. 'I shall call Kristýna and tell her to wait for us on the outskirts of the city. We can leave this car there and she'll take us to No. 53. Then we can leave Karla with her, if she agrees.'

It was just as well that the journey down the motorway passed off quietly, because Tomáš would not have been able to take any more adrenalin. Nobody spoke much as they perhaps came to terms with the awful events of the day. He still could not believe it had all happened.

Kristýna was already waiting for them at the parking lot. She was calm and composed as always. She asked no questions and headed off for the centre straight away. In the meantime Karla had changed out of her prison clothes, which they ripped up and threw into a backstreet container. It was late evening when they arrived home. Before they got out of the car, Tomáš launched into them. 'What the bloody hell are we doing? Are you in your right minds? I am not going upstairs. I don't want to have anything to do with this!'

Dimitri tried to talk him round. 'We've not actually done anything wrong. Remember? That man wasn't killed by Karla, and she's been wrongly imprisoned anyway. Do at least come upstairs with us. You'll see it'll all get sorted out.'

Kristýna did not say anything, but just looked at him sympathetically. If he had not felt that same urge he had had in the mountains when he decided to go back to see Kohl, he would not have agreed, though he was still reproaching himself on the stairs.

2/16 Dream future

As Tomáš closed the creaking door behind him, he started speaking straight away.

'Are you aware what we have done? I do not understand you! We are helping an escaped convict. We are putting ourselves and our families in danger. Bloody hell! Don't you see?'

'Get a grip, Tom,' said Marek. 'When will you finally understand that keeping to the rules does not mean the same as doing the right thing?'

'Leave it out, you two,' said Dimitri. 'You won't get anywhere by bickering. We can deal with this quietly.'

Tomáš exploded: 'I am not going to be told what's right and wrong by some little idiot. A fine mess I have got myself in!' His intake of breath was too brief for anybody else to get a word in edgeways: 'Quietly? How am I to be quiet? We are in the same room as a murderer who is being sought all over the country. We are helping her to escape. My baby is due in two weeks, and I might not be there because they're gonna put me in jail!'

'Am I supposed to act as if I haven't heard anything? You don't have to help me. I'll just look after myself as always. Good-bye.' So saying, Karla took the bag of Kristýna's things and moved towards the door.

Marek started to get furious. 'You're just exaggerating for no reason, you fool! Nobody is going to put you away. Don't act so yellow. And you stay here, Karla.'

This was too much! He clenched his fist and might have punched him if Kristýna had not spoken up. 'Your emotions are quite in order, but please don't let them take over. This has not happened by chance.' They started shouting over each other, but Dimitri silenced them.

'You've had your turn. Now let Kristýna speak.'

She spoke calmly and quietly. 'Now all four of you are very much lacking in energy. You have been through a really tough day today. But let's not forget why we are here. We can only accomplish our task if we remain united. It doesn't matter what any one of us did in the past. Do you think it's just by chance that there was a riot and Karla escaped just at the moment you were visiting her? Your fears are now stopping you from seeing the way we have to go. They are preventing you from seeing with your hearts. Please stay with us, Karla. We need you.'

Karla put her bag of clothes on the floor and nodded.

Tomáš quietened down and felt really exhausted. His entire body was stiff, and somehow he was hungry, yet had no appetite for food. We would have most liked to crawl into bed somewhere and sleep. He asked in a muted tone, 'But what if it all turns out wrong? What if we should not be here at all? How can we tell the difference?'

'Ah, Doubting Tomáš calling,' Dimitri quipped with some hyperbole.

'As soon as we restore our energy, everything will get sorted out, I promise,' said Kristýna. 'Now all of you sit down in a circle and I shall light the candles.' The way she said this reminded Tomáš of Kohl and the way he always spoke to him. These thoughts raised his energy a little.

Karla and Marek looked astonished. They did not understand how this energy restoration could help them at all, but they did what was required of them. Tomáš's day had been so full of surprises that this one was not going to put him out. It was all somehow the same to him now. Soon they were sitting in a circle around lit candles and incense sticks. Kristýna turned off all the lights, returned to her place and spoke quietly:

'Please close your eyes and move into your hearts.' After a period of silence she continued. 'Close your eyes and open your heart. Stop perceiving the external noise and focus on your inner self. Breathe in slowly and breathe out slowly, like the ebb and flow of the tide in the ocean. Perceive those enormous oceans within yourself. The waves gradually wash away the fear and apprehension of what will be. Slowly breathe in and slowly breathe out, as the wind murmurs through the leaves of the trees. Perceive the great mountains within yourself. The wind slowly bears off all anger and feelings of guilt that have piled up in your heart. Slowly breathe in and slowly breathe out and imagine a sun emerging. You are that sun. The light that you radiate penetrates into all corners of the universe. Perceive the endless universe. Perceive its beauty here and now. Now relinquish everything. Only your true self will remain.'

It was difficult to tell how long it lasted, but it was one of the most beautiful states he had ever experienced. Again he discovered that wonderful world within himself. He felt his heart opening fully. He did not know if he was dreaming or not, but he heard Kristýna telling a tale about a little soul that became the light. In order to know what it is to be the light, she first had to know the darkness, a darkness so deep that for a moment she forgot she was the light. Tomáš very much enjoyed this sense of union and awakening. He forgot about what had been and what was to be. Now he simply was. He fully perceived his soul, his life going round within and his heart beating. He felt himself to be so alive! From somewhere far off he heard:

'Now you may slowly open your eyes.'

He guessed from the burnt-down candles that it had lasted half an hour or perhaps an hour. His energy level was now so high that he could sense the evaporation of his previous blocks, prejudices and false impressions of the world, some of them many years old. Then he focused on the people in the room. Something about them had changed. It was as if an enormous burden had been lifted from them. Dimitri's facial features, which he had not previously noticed, were now very prominent. He looked so wise. Marek exuded self-assurance and decisiveness. Kristýna looked even fresher than she usually did. Karla had lost the circles beneath her eyes and regained a normal complexion. Tomáš put her at ten years younger. Even her protruding ears now struck him as sexy. Amazing how a murderer can turn into a model in such a short time, he thought. Impulsively he said:

'I do apologize for calling you a murderer, Karla. I don't actually believe that you did it.'

Tears welled up in her eyes and it was not long before she was shaking all over and sobbing. Kristýna sat beside her and began stroking her back. All the stress, despair and sense of inferiority that had eaten away at her in prison now had to come out. Tomáš slowly realized just how hard it had been for her. She had lost her family and friends overnight. Only the most loyal remained.

She had felt it to be an enormous injustice when they had sentenced her for killing a man. She was the kind of person who would never intentionally harm anybody, and yet they had put her in prison for something as despicable as shooting a fugitive in the back. He could feel the anger that had choked her for years and literally kept her awake at night, slowly gnawing away at her and destroying her from within. Now it was all floating to the surface and slowly evaporating. Still in tears, she said to Kristýna, 'Thank you for not asking if I really did it.' Then she wiped her red eyes and smiled for the first time. 'Thank you, all. I was never meant to get out of that prison. Now I have been given a second chance. I feel freer than I have ever felt before. I didn't intend to help you. I just wanted to use you, so that you'd hide me, but now I have the feeling that I am in the right place among the right people. Whatever needs to be done, I shall help you.'

Marek, who would have thought the same way in her situation, admitted:

'I took the whole thing to be a fun trip, but now I see it differently. This is about something big. Now I am glad to be involved.'

'Next time you don't have much energy, then remember that as of today you are firmly earthed and your hearts are open above,' said Kristýna.

'I hope there won't be a next time,' Tomáš commented.

'Amen,' Marek added, and everyone started laughing.

'Firstly I want to explain to Karla,' said Dimitri, 'just why we were looking for her. About a month ago Naďa contacted me and said she wanted to do an interview with me about my book. She also told me straight away that an important task awaited me. She described each of you as people I would not be able to do it without. She said we'd come together in any case after enough time had passed, but that we didn't have the time to wait. Karla, you were the last member of the team and today we just tried to contact you. We had no idea at all how it would all turn out.'

'None of us know all the background – just snippets here and there. Now if we follow our intuition we can put together the picture and the role that we play in it.'

Karla was more down-to-earth. 'We have to agree not to meet up for some time. It would be too dangerous. I think a month will do. In any case you're going to have your hands full enough, changing nappies, Tom.' This amused everyone, but then she grew more serious: 'They're probably going to summons all three of you to appear for questioning. Your testimonies can vary, but they should match on key points. It might be best if you say I forced you to get in the car and that you were my hostages. I took your mobile phones and money and set you down somewhere in the forest. When they ask why you didn't try to escape it will do to say you were simply afraid. They might ridicule you, considering one woman abducted three lads, but you can survive that.'

'I'm not sure I'll survive that! I can get you some forged documents, but you're going to have to hide somewhere for a couple of days,' said Marek.

'I'd also like to tell Karla what we know so far about our task,' said Dimitri. 'It's something to do with the crisis that the world is currently going through. For a long time the politicians have not admitted that something is going wrong. They probably knew, but they preferred not to talk about it. Most people shared this voluntary ignorance with them. We did not want to admit the truth, so we preferred to lie about it to ourselves all the time. We lied to ourselves that humanity is improving every day and developing. We lied to ourselves that in spite of all the differences between the races, nations and various religions we could at least agree on basic things – basic issues like adequate food and drinking water for everybody regardless of origin. We tried to convince ourselves that we're human beings who are able to sacrifice a little luxury so that others don't die of hunger.'

'That is what is weighing us down so very much deep inside,' said Kristýna. 'We know that the world we are living in does not match our expectations. We know things shouldn't look this way. Humanity has long kept up the same lifestyle and the same way of thinking, in the hope that things would turn out for the better. Several years ago there came a turning point. Enough people realized that something wasn't right and that humanity was spitting in its own face – enough people to start a change in social, political and economic life. This was working out fine, until just recently,' she sighed. 'Something I cannot describe in detail has started to impede us. I think our task will be to do something about this. Our task is to help other people to turn the world into a more beautiful and just place to live. Last week Naďa said that our team has the specific task of stopping one man who is going to stand in the way of this transformation. She says this man meant a lot to you, Karla. Perhaps it's your father or a former lover.'

Karla looked surprised. 'I don't know who that might be. Of all the men that meant anything to me there wasn't anybody interested in doing any harm.'

Tomáš thought something wasn't right here. 'Hold on a minute. As a teacher I've learnt to remember exactly what people say. Naďa never said it's a man who meant a lot to you, but a man who has played an important role in your life, Karla.'

Now Karla's face was full of anger and hatred. 'I've never met a worse swine in my life than Musílek. He manipulates people and he's only interested in power. When I was his partner he used to tell me how he would get into power and the whole world would lie at his feet. I took it all with a smile, before he had me sent to jail and then moved on to be Deputy Police Commissioner.'

Marek frowned. 'He won't stay Deputy for long. I got word today that the current Police Commissioner is stepping down and Musílek is going to replace him.'

'Why didn't you say anything, Marek?'

'It didn't strike me as important.'

Dimitri furrowed his brow. 'Everything here is important! If we are going to succeed we have to tell each other everything. Does anybody else have any 'unimportant' information to pass on?'

A silence descended. For a while Tomáš hesitated as everything within him boiled over. He stammered a word or two. Everybody turned round and looked at him enquiringly, and everybody said what they all had on the tip of their tongue. 'What is it, Tomáš? What do you want to tell us?'

He brought to mind the state of carefree union that he had experienced just some time previously. This filled him with energy, so he took a deep breath and started talking.

'I have these dreams. These dreams show me where the situation is heading. The present-day confusion is being used by people who have no respect for life and who are whipping up the masses. It's going to be a lot worse that I ever thought. I don't know just how true dreams can be.'

'What do you see in these dreams exactly?'

'The whole world in the grip of war. Nuclear weapons falling everywhere. It's a bit different each time, as if it's not clear how it will happen exactly. People will be living insecurely like rats underground. They won't trust each other, as chaos and despair take hold everywhere. Modern, sophisticated concentration camps will be set up for those who cannot adapt and those held responsible for what is happening. Various dictators and religious leaders will murder all those who don't agree with them in the name of their truths. Recently I've been having my dreams almost every night. I don't know if anything like that can really happen at all. And I apologize for not telling you earlier, but I just took them to be nightmares.'

He felt relieved. Silence fell over the room, disturbed only by the noise from the street. Everyone seemed to understand what their task was, why Naďa had contacted them and why the events in the prison had happened.

The first to speak up was Dimitri, even though he himself did not know what to say. 'Well, I never imagined in my wildest dreams that it would be up to us to avert something like this, and that it was within our power at all...'

'I don't like all this apocalyptical-sounding nonsense at all,' said Marek. 'And even if it were true, what can six people do to change the whole world?'

This did not seem to put Kristýna off her stride at all. 'If the world is moving towards a Third World War, then we have to stop it basically by not allowing Musílek to get into power. Let us not even try to deal with the problem as a whole. Let us just deal with what we can see – just like when you're driving a car at night, Marek. You can only see two hundred metres in front of you, as far as your lights shine. As for Tomáš's dreams, I have the feeling we won't be too far off all that soon.' And as it was Kristýna who was saying this, Tomáš's throat tightened.

Dimitri's thoughts seemed to be completely elsewhere and he appeared to be speaking in a trance, but he still fittingly commented, 'It is only when facing the abyss that people will be able to change. Only if they are staring doom in the face. The system is no longer fit for purpose – it's out of date. It will have to fall, and from its ashes will rise a new, more just world. My guess is that it is up to us to make sure the system is reconstructed without violence. At least in our own country. Tomáš's dreams must not come true. Perhaps they are not actually impending, but for us they will always provide a certain incentive. What you see, Tom, is not the future, but just a raised finger. It is what we have to avoid.'

Marek was ready with a comment as always: 'Just so long as that raised finger is not a raised middle finger.'

Tomáš was surprised at just how decently he expressed himself. He usually chose spicier expressions, but now he was being quite matter-of-fact.

'I don't think there's going to be an apocalypse, even though some people might want one. Humanity has been here for a long time and will be here for a long time to come. That doesn't mean I'm naive when it comes to human nature, of course. When things get tough, people will do what they have to to get their way. It would not be the first time that the charismatic lunatics started swarming round and abusing ordinary people. I agree that power within the system is now being redistributed. That always bears risks. It doesn't take much for violence to become the norm.'

'You're right, Marek. People can easily substitute a feeling of security for a sense of compassion.'

Kristýna was focusing on a different idea, but only to get at the solution from a different angle. 'Politicians, bankers and ordinary people are afraid they aren't going to be needed any more. What's wrong with that? We are all like this: I have to go as far as I'm needed, both by my family and by society. There is nothing remarkable about being kind towards people when I'm compelling them to form a dependence upon me. We all have to exert all our efforts to ensure that those around us will no longer need us. Our little ego is afraid of this, but that is the way to go. That is the fulfilment of our objective. We must not be afraid that people are no longer going to need us. If we overcome this fear, a new task will always emerge after a period of emptiness. A new task! We will always be needed. It needs to be explained to people that the end of one system does not automatically mean they aren't going to be needed any more.' Tomáš pondered over what she had just said. It was the profound and pure truth. Nobody had ever explained it to him like that before.

'Well I think that is an entirely sound conclusion,' Dimitri assessed the discussion. 'At least we can make do with it until a specific task emerges. I shall join you when we have our next meeting. We should stop meeting for some time now, as Karla said. It will be safer that way.'

He rose from his chair and headed for the corridor. Only Karla and Kristýna remained in the room. As he was putting his coat on, Dimitri turned to Tomáš and Marek and said, 'Don't forget that the police will be in touch with us soon. Try to look the part.'

Tomáš was much more pensive than usual on his way home, his thoughts revolving around the situation in the prison and the subsequent escape. He realized how low his energy level had been, and now he had enough energy he saw things completely differently and with detachment. I will have to watch out for that next time, he thought, admitting: today I was definitely not acting like a catalyst. Again he felt ashamed and had to laugh at himself. He was also surprised by something else: the enormous difference in his view of one and the same thing depending on his energy level. In this case, Karla. With a low energy level she was a murderer and with a high energy level she was a team member he was concerned about.

He felt an enormous sense of relief that he had told them all about his dreams. On the other hand he was quite put out that the others had not immediately demolished the idea. Perhaps he had been lying to himself when he said they were just nightmares that had nothing to do with reality. Each time he always breathed a sigh of relief and slowly realized that it was just a dream. This always calmed him down. But what now?

— • —

Tomáš went to the police the very next day. He raised his energy level just before the interview, but he was sucked dry quite soon. Perhaps it's not them – perhaps it's just the place, he thought. He subsequently realized that one of the police officers reminded him of his father, which made him feel better immediately. Suddenly he did not feel so remote from them. Even though their questions were particularly intrusive, they were quite decent about it, and they did not seem to have any suspicions. The questioning lasted about half an hour. At the end they got round to talking about the expected baby. This rather mollified the police and they wished him all the best for the birth.

2/17 The miracle

Again the sun rose a couple of minutes earlier than on the previous day. Summer was approaching. The warming morning light penetrated the blinds. It was Saturday, so Tomáš did not have to go into work. It was going to be a Saturday like any other. He stretched and immediately went into the kitchen to make breakfast for Eliška and the baby. It was a week after the due date. The best-laid plans... he thought, and smiled as he poured the tea. He waited for the butter to soften a little on the bread roll so he could spread it, when she started shouting from the bedroom, 'It's here. Start the car up, dear!'

He dropped the knife on the floor and quickly ran into the bedroom, almost colliding with the table. He took the laid-out coat and helped her to dress. She was smiling, but he could tell she was rather nervous. She sat on the back seat and they set off for the hospital. For a long time he had played this scene over in his mind. The lights were on green at most crossroads and there were no traffic jams – as if it were all directed from above.

He did not want to attend the birth as he could not bear the sight of blood. Eliška knew this very well and never once hinted a reproach. He was with her all the time she had her contractions. He held her hand and told her one joke after another, until she was actually having the contractions, when he shut up just to be sure. After a while there was not much room for jokes and a little after that they took her to the delivery room. He waited for them to call him there. About two hours later a nurse came for him.

'Come with me please, Mr Jedlička.'

They passed through several doors and the time he had dreamed of for so long had finally arrived. Eliška was half sitting up in bed, holding their baby in her arms. She looked so exhausted and yet so happy. When she saw him she gave him a tired smile:

'It's a girl. So here's Věrka. See how beautiful she is!'

He just stood there and could not say very much. After a while he walked up to the bed, where he was greeted by the most beautiful sight in the world. The baby was wrapped in a blanket and had her eyes closed. Her little pink head was happily pressed against her mother's breast. She looked so vulnerable. Everything that Kohl had said to him about parenthood now came back to mind. He was not sure he would manage to give Věrka everything she would need, but whatever her dreams might be, he would do everything to be able to make them come true. He would always protect her, laugh with her when she was happy and hold her hand when she felt bad.

The baby slowly opened her eyes and blinked several times: 'Eheh!'

She was so marvellous he melted completely. He had never seen Eliška so happy. He recalled the day the doctor told them they could never have children. This broke her. There is nothing worse than seeing your loved one lose her dreams, he thought. As he watched her now with Věrka in her arms, the tears welled up in his eyes. Now he was just thinking one thought:

'Thank you.'

He wanted to ask if it hurt, but then he realized what a stupid question that was.

They looked at each other and did not say anything. There was no need for words. It was a unique moment. The kind that simply and suddenly comes to pass, and you stand in dumb amazement at how beautiful the world is. Tomáš realized that life cannot be described in any way at all. It dawned on him: If we had to describe it we would have to remain silent, and he just looked on. This suddenly opened up a great mystery to him – that he should think about life less and live it more. This was confirmed by his soul: *Don't try to understand life, just live it.*

He had the most fantastic family in the world and he was appropriately proud of them. He felt like shouting out to the whole world: This is my wonderful wife, and the most fantastic daughter in the world has been born to us. He noticed that on her left cheek she had a cute birthmark, a little freckle. He attempted to stroke her as gently as possible and touched her for the first time.

'She's so tiny,' and he looked into Eliška's eyes.

'Well, she definitely didn't strike me as tiny when she came out.'

Both of them had forgotten about time completely. The nurse came to the bed and apologized that she now had to take her for an examination, and that the newly fledged mother had to rest. She took the baby very carefully in her arms, held her head and walked towards the door. She did this with total love and humility.

— • —

The following month was the best yet in Tomáš's life. After a few days the girls came out of hospital, once he had made the final alterations in the baby's room. It wasn't actually necessary, but he felt like doing it. The baby would meanwhile sleep in a cot with them in their bedroom. He had arranged two weeks' holiday, so he could be at home with his family. Although he had held the baby in his arms a couple of times at the hospital, he still did not feel entirely confident holding her. He was afraid he might hurt her, but after a few days he became more self-assured.

He returned to the energy levels that he had enjoyed together with Kohl. He felt life pulsing though him and his soul moving within him. It was very pleasant: *I am always with you. I was with you when you were first together with Kohl, and I will be with you when you succeed in your effort to change the world.*

He had the feeling he could embrace the whole world. Again he was aware just how many wonderful souls there were all around him. How much light. However, he was also able to better identify the people who only wanted to suck him dry. He had learnt how to deal with them. Whenever anybody tried it on, he connected with his soul and immediately replaced the depleted energy. He tried this out when he bumped into a woman in a shop, who was shouting at everybody in a dreadful way, quite beside herself with rage. He had never heard anybody yelling that much. He caught hold of a shopping trolley that she had furiously thrust to one side, and tried to calm her down, but he should not have. The woman began pouring out all her anger on him and vulgarly swearing at him. For a time he had the urge to defend himself – it was awfully difficult to resist, but then he breathed in deep, apologized to the woman with a smile and walked away. She was left standing there astonished. She was no longer shouting.

— • —

Life became rather more difficult when he started going back to work. There were nights when he barely caught a wink of sleep. His colleagues and pupils tolerated his micro-siestas and made fun of him:

'Just as well you don't drive for a living, Tom.'

One lesson the 4A kids made him tell them what it was like to be a father.

'It's hard to describe,' he said cautiously, but after a short silence he did take the plunge.

'All the time you imagine parenthood a certain way and you prepare yourself for it, and then it looks completely different.'

The whole class laughed, though of course there was no holding Dominik back. 'And how does it actually look?'

He sat on the table as he always did when he was expounding:

'It's a load of detail. You have to learn to be cautious, but you can't do things by halves. You can't take time off and go off for a beer with the lads. You might be able to later, but not now. The baby needs all your attention. You find out that all those things that used to be so very important are no longer important at all. Strangely, even though it's an enormous responsibility, you do it all automatically anyway. You don't have to force yourself to do anything. It doesn't even bother you to get up seven times a night because she's crying. It's true that now I'm feeling sleepy and I feel like cursing, but somewhere inside I feel enormously thankful for it all.'

After he had earned numerous glances of recognition, some tears from the girls and an expression of absolute disgust from Robert, he asked his pupils, 'And what are your parents like?'

Beáta sighed: 'Sometimes I have the feeling that mine want me to be someone completely different. Their sentences often start with "You ought to..."'

Dominik was better off: 'I like my folks a lot – I wouldn't change them for anyone, but sometimes they do really annoy me, because they plan every moment of my life. Every weekend we have to go somewhere and we have to have some kind of experience. Sometimes I'd just like to lie in front of the TV set or read my comics.'

'You're doing fine, Dominik. My folks are hardly interested in me,' Kamila said. 'Mum's always working in her salon, and dad comes home from work, sits in front of the TV and doesn't do a thing. Nobody chats with me. It's too bad I don't actually have any brothers or sisters,' she complained.

'Right, that reminds me of my dad,' said Beáta. 'He's an awful brute. He doesn't show his emotions at all. I always thought that men are just like that, but thank God I've found a great boyfriend. He's not afraid to show his emotions. And he's no sissy either. He's just right.'

Some of the other pupils complained about their parents. What bothered them most was that they often made it clear to them what their expectations were. If they did something different in life then there was always the danger they would fall out of favour with them. Roman added, 'My folks are cool. They don't try to make me into somebody different. My mum is like my best mate.'

Martin felt bad because he thought his parents had broken up over him. 'Mum wanted me to do what I enjoy in life. Dad wanted me to be heterosexual.'

Tomáš pointed out his error. 'A child can neither destroy nor save a marriage. Your parents are mature adults, and you cannot force them to do anything. And vice versa.'

After he had heard them all out he described his own. 'My father wanted me to be a car mechanic. For a long time I sought the strength in myself to be able to tell him that I wanted to be a teacher. When I eventually confided in him, he didn't take it very well. For several weeks he barely spoke to me. He had always expected me to take over his workshop. But then I was helped a lot during that time by my grandad: 'Aye, ever since 'ee were a yung 'un 'ee allus liked sulkin' a lot, but 'ee allus gorrover it,' and things did turn out okay after that. In fact we have got on a lot better ever since. I think he respects me for being able to go my own way. It also helped him when he saw that I enjoy my work as a teacher and that it fulfils me.'

After a moment of silence, Robert raised his hand. Tomáš was on the point of nipping his attempt to make an inappropriate remark in the bud, but something told him he'd better be quiet this time.

'My folks want me to be an architect. They have my life all marked out in advance. Both of them are well-known architects. When I told them I wanted to be a footballer, they made fun of me: 'You won't make a living that way!' and 'Your career will end when you're thirty-five. And what will you do then?! You're not up to it anyway!' Ever since I've had to accept I'm going to have to do what they want. But deep down I still dream of being a famous footballer. I train three times a week and I'm one of the best players on the team. My parents have never come to watch a match. They're ashamed of me. They wanted an educated architect in a suit and they have a sportsman in a sweaty tracksuit. Do you think I should put up more of a fight against them, sir?'

Tomáš had overcome his initial shock when Robert spoke to him seriously for the first time in his life and he heard the click as if the points in his mind had switched.

'Definitely!'

'But I get the feeling I don't have a choice,' and Robert lowered his eyes.

'You always have a choice!' and looking him straight in the eyes he kindled a spark of hope in them.

In the afternoon he switched on the news and played with the baby on the sofa. Suddenly he dropped everything and sat up in astonishment, as a report came on that Police Commissioner Musílek had stepped down from office. For the first time Tomáš saw what he actually looked like. He had an athletic figure, with an expensive jacket fitting perfectly over his large shoulders and filled out to the final millimetre with an enormous chest. His short hair and smoothly shaven face made his prominent cheek bones stand out even more. In a brief statement with passion in his eyes he gave the reasons for his resignation.

'I am disgusted by the current situation in this country. The system is corrupt and rotten. For a long time I have tried to change it. I have asked for help from the Interior Minister, but he has just ignored my request. I have realized that all my efforts have been in vain, so I have stepped down from my position as Police Commissioner.'

Tomáš did not know what to think. Around seven he received a text message from Dimitri, asking him to take part in another meeting at five on Wednesday at No. 53. After thinking it over for a little while he wrote back that he would be there.

2/18 What if?

Over a month had passed since the events at the prison. Whenever Tomáš thought back to them a chill ran down his spine and he was gripped by terror. And yet he looked forward to meeting up with Dimitri, Kristýna, Jirka, Marek and Karla again at No. 53. He was among the first to arrive. Without realizing it he talked about Věrka almost all the time. He described how he felt when the baby was born and did not leave out any of his first amusing anecdotes.

'I'm always a little unsure,' he finally added.

Jirka knew very well what he was talking about. 'As a parent you can never be entirely sure, believe me.'

When the others had arrived, Marek took the floor first. 'I have obtained some information about the prison riot. It was probably all planned by Karel Hrdlička and Josef Brada, who are both multiple murderers. The good news is that the police aren't accusing Karla of taking part in the riot. The video recordings clearly show she didn't know anything in advance. And the best is yet to come: as she was inside for involuntary manslaughter and she didn't harm her hostages, she is not in the same risk category as armed fugitives, so basically, catching Karla is not a big police priority right now.'

'Oh, that's marvellous,' Dimitri rejoiced, though wrinkles had formed around his temples. Karla, who was listening tensely, leant back in her armchair in relief. Kristýna wandered off for a while and brought back freshly brewed tea and her biscuits from the kitchen in a beautiful hand-painted bowl, so this time it was Marek who rejoiced.

'And that's not all! The cops don't suspect any of us of 'elpin' Karla to escape. And you'll enjoy this: Tomáš's file even mentions 'e's expectin' a wee nipper.'

They all laughed at this, as Tomáš realized he sometimes talked too much.

Jirka did not neglect to have a dig. 'Better not ask where you get this kind of information from, Marek.'

'I wouldn't tell you anyway. I protect my sources like all good journalists. Unfortunately, I've got some bad news too. I found a couple of things on Musílek. For example, some people who've got in his way were shot by a burglar, or had a car accident.'

A chill ran down Tomáš's spine. After a period of silence Karla spoke up. 'I think I should tell you all what actually happened on the night that crook was shot. Musílek and I were on a night shift. I never did like him much, but I always thought it was my fault and that he was probably an acquired taste. The bastard!' There was not the least doubt that her hatred for him was deadly. 'When we arrived at the scene we heard some kind of noise in a nearby street. We ran over to look, and the crook was trying to get into a parked car. When he saw us he started to run. He didn't respond to challenges, so I shot into the air, and at that moment he stood stock still. He had just started to turn round when Musílek shot him right in the back. I yelled at him, but he defended himself by saying the crook was going to shoot us. When we ran up to him, he examined him, but didn't find a weapon on him. I remember Musílek's face when he realized what he'd done. He argued with me for a while and made endless promises, including promotion, if I said what he wanted. When I refused he turned on me and I'll never forget till the end of my life what he said. "You're going to regret that, girl". Another patrol arrived. As soon as they found that our testimonies did not basically match they took our guns. Musílek said he was the one who shot into the air, and I was the one who shot the crook.'

Jirka could not believe this. 'But what about the ballistics tests? They must have found that the gun that fired the shot wasn't yours.'

Karla closed her eyes and put her hand to her face. 'This is the part that I don't understand. The tests did indicate it was my gun that fired the shot.'

'Now I do understand that perfectly, because I found that the person in charge of the ballistics testing is now in a very high position, and often plays golf with our former Police Commissioner.'

The time had arrived for a question that Tomáš had been pondering all morning. 'I saw that on television. It doesn't seem right to me. Musílek strikes me very much as a man who yearns for power, and yet he has stepped down?'

Again Jirka was on top of this. 'This is actually meant to launch his political career. Okay this is second-hand info, but according to good friends of mine who move in political circles, Musílek is getting ready to move in. The fact that he stepped down from office in this way is meant to draw attention to himself, so he collects political points.'

'That makes sense,' said Dimitri. 'It shows his sophistication and determination. It makes even more sense to me now that we have Karla on the team.'

However, Karla had her doubts. 'He's too much of a prat for people to listen to him. He's not all there in the head.'

'If he offers people solutions to their problems, then that is not going to bother them. The worst thing we could do now is underrate him,' said Jirka.

'Well, I still can't believe that anybody might want to follow him,' said Karla.

Kristýna, who had so far been listening attentively, went along with Jirka. 'He's up to something. No one like him would give up such a strong position without planning to attain a much higher one. If we put it all together with the fact that life is going to keep getting worse and might even move towards what Tomáš sees in his dreams, then we are facing a real problem.'

'Of course, the elections are not for another two years,' said Jirka, 'and the present government is quite stable, so he doesn't have too many opportunities to get into power.'

Kristýna said something that did not cheer Tomáš up at all. 'Let us be entirely honest with ourselves. The current situation puts us closer to a conflict like that than ever before.'

Marek put his empty plate on the table and wiped the sides of his mouth. 'Everything indicates it's gonna get worse.'

Everybody looked at him in surprise, with the same thing in mind as Dimitri:

'Last time you were basically very much against any apocalyptical theories.'

'That's true,' he admitted, 'but I've taken a bit more interest lately. It isn't too difficult to see that something is on the cards. You just have to put two and two together from info online.' Five pairs of eyes observed him enquiringly without blinking.

'Data such as the extent to which the number of searches for strings with the words 'war', 'end of the world', 'dictatorship' and 'violence' has increased.'

This struck Tomáš as very much to be regretted. 'I cannot believe people could stoop so low again. Look around at how people look after each other everywhere.'

Dimitri put on a carewor expression. 'Over seven billion people live on this planet. What is going to happen to them when they lose control of their emotions, or they're overwhelmed by fear? What if the worst in us comes out on top?'

'In these days of modern mass media, we're not taken in by some lunatic that easily. Everything can be verified online...' but then Marek fell silent for a while.

'Unless they believe it of them because there's no access to the information. Even now opinions are circulating among the experts that the internet is growing too fast. It's so enormous and everything within it just loops back into itself. All it takes is a small poke in the right place and it will all collapse like a house of cards, followed by the collapse of the entire infrastructure.'

Tomáš now felt sick in his stomach. His head began to buzz and he almost fainted. It was all just too much for him. He repeated 'I love you' to himself several times until the feeling that enveloped him like a straightjacket vanished as quickly as it had appeared.

After the others had made sure he was all right, Dimitri carried on the discussion.

'The banking system is breaking down, the media are going to stop functioning. State administration will break down across the globe. States will gradually begin to divide into smaller and smaller territorial units. Even these days separatist and nationalist sentiments are making themselves felt in various countries. And it's in this kind of situation that people can get so desperate, they're susceptible to various dogmatic leaders' views. When people are afraid they are going to lose everything then they listen to anybody who promises to look after them.'

Now Tomáš was reminded of what Kristýna had been saying previously. He decided to round off her idea. 'People are afraid of what the future might bring. They're afraid they won't be needed under the new system. They're apprehensive that when the system is reconstructed there will be violence and chaos. They are terrified of losing the security they already have. Most of those fears are actually unjustified – people are still going to be needed, and we will always find a reason to exist. However, the fears of violence are justified, as are those of the loss of security. We are going to have to give up a lot of the things we think we must have in life, but then that will help us to realize that we really only need a little to carry on the way we have been doing. If people can get their egos under control and put their souls in charge then this will work out. When you connect yourself firmly with the earth and yet remain entirely open upwards then you will see everything clearly. You will feel how painful this transformation will be, but you will also recognize that it must take place. Humanity will not perish. It will be a complicated birth, but whatever emerges will be worth it. What is today a majority, with its lying, pretence and power struggles, will become a minority to remind us of what the world used to be like.'

Dimitri could not conceal his enthusiasm. 'Ah, that is what I call a true catalyst! Bravo, Tom. But then how can people be persuaded not to be afraid and to do what their souls advise them? What do you think, Jirka? You know how to get at them.'

'Basically, people need more imagination. Today it is easier to imagine the end of the world than the end of the current system. They need to be persuaded that the world is not going to end and that they'll be better off under the new system. They're afraid of the unknown, so let us describe to them what is going to emerge. Against us there are various demagogues who will tell them between the lines that they are needed. The change actually means that the new order will have far more elements of democracy than previously. People were not previously prepared for this, but now they are. We no longer need anybody behind our back for us to behave decently. We don't need to observe any Ten Commandments or anything like that. All you need to do is listen to your conscience. In future they will talk about our times as the age of enslavement.'

Tomáš was now feeling very well, and he had no difficulty formulating highly complex thoughts. 'People need to be shown that if they remain united they will no longer need to seek differences and they can focus on the common profit, so that truly everybody will reap the rewards, and significant progress will be made as a result. Substantially more progress than if we are each doing our own thing. The greatest progress in the history of humanity.'

'Not only show them what unity is, but let them experience it,' said Kristýna.

Karla remembered the meditation she had performed with Kristýna just before the meeting that day. For the first time she had experienced union with everything. 'We have to explain to people that evil begets evil. We all have to understand that during this greatest of crises it is vitally important to preserve our sense of compassion. Not pity but compassion. This means you are not going to feel sorry for someone or make a poor cripple out of him. Compassion is when you show him that he is not on his own and you encourage him to seek out his own talent. People will then stop being afraid of ending up redundant.'

Kristýna was generous with her praise. 'Excellent, Karla. I can see that our joint meditations and chats are beginning to pay off. If we

forget compassion, we can survive as a species, but not as humanity.'

'I can understand your interest in resolvin' the global crisis, but
wouldn't it do just for starters to stop Musílek?' Marek quipped, making everyone laugh.

2/19 Lost

For a long time Tomáš could not fall asleep, so he got up and went
to get a drink of water. The kitchen was flooded with moon-
light, as a full moon was floating on high right above the attic window, which gave this sleepless night a very odd atmosphere.
Crack, he hit the glass against the side of the sink and it smashed.
Half-asleep, he clattered around the kitchen range. Damn, where is
it?! he thought. After a couple of minutes he found what he was looking for. He put the glasses box next to the waste basket, and at last
he could go back to bed and at least try to sleep. Eliška was sleeping
peacefully, while Věrka was tossing and turning a little. He observed
her for a while to make sure she was all right. She seemed to be, so he
stretched out in bed again and then rolled from side to side in an effort
to quieten his restless thoughts.

For a moment he lost consciousness and for a while after that he
felt he was falling, terrified that he would come to the end of his fall.
He prayed for it to end, for him to fall down and end this horror,
but he kept falling and his terror turned into torment. When he hit
frozen-solid ground he had the wind knocked right out of him and
gasped for breath. He had the feeling this lasted for hours. Finally he
managed to turn on his belly and catch his breath. He immediately
recognized where he was from the stale smell of the floor. He would
have recognized that obtrusive stench anywhere. He was still lying

on his belly and felt awful, as if his innards had been stuck in a mixer turned on full. His lungs clammed up, his heart thumped cruelly and his head throbbed so much he felt like smashing it against a wall just to forget the pain for a while. He did not even have the strength to cry out. Only a long time after he stopped vomiting and bleeding from the nose could he regain control of his sphincters and the torment began to recede, though he felt he was losing a substantial part of himself at the same time. He was confused and tired, and felt like sleeping. How he wanted to sleep! For some time he tried to meditate and waited for it to get better, but it did not.

Perhaps on the third attempt he managed to stand up, his ribs ached and his head was spinning. At every step his sore feet could be heard, as if he had two steel brushes for soles. He looked around, feeling a sharp pain with each movement of the neck. He found himself in a connecting corridor, which must have been somewhere in the northern part of the shelter, because not so much water could be kept on the surface and most of the other parts were already flooded. Soon most of the complex would be uninhabitable. Behind him he heard a noise and decided to head off in that direction. As he approached, a woman's groans could be heard. Out of curiosity he went to see what was happening.

In the half-collapsed tunnel with streams of water pouring down from the roof he gradually made out three figures. On the ground there lay a woman, who was groaning in a shrill voice. A man who was as fat as a pig was gratifying himself upon her, while the entire act was being watched by a gaunt, slathering man. Before Tomáš decided to move on elsewhere, for some time he observed the victim trying to free herself. Eventually she gave up. He walked into a dark alleyway, where the groaning gradually subsided. He tripped over something and fell sprawling all over it. Abrasions had previously been missing from his list of injuries apparently. His nostrils were then invaded by that stench, and he realized he had just fallen over a corpse. He stood up with difficulty, wiped his dirty hands and walked on. He could not keep his eyes open and yet he could not sleep. He had the feeling he had not slept for months and he could hardly lift his legs.

He began to recognize his surroundings. It was Section A, near the local police station. The man at the temporary gatehouse was just injecting his arm with some drug. It was all the same to him that Tomáš walked past him. When he got to the station complex itself he heard a shout and some other noise from the little street to the right.

As he got nearer he started to make out individual sounds. The constant rattle and banging of sheet metal was occasionally accompanied by men's shouts:

'You show him! Rip his balls off!'

While another one yelled:

'Bite him properly. I wanna see meat!'

Their voices were a mixture of anger and excitement. When he got there, one man was shouting, 'Now die, you swine!'

The stench of blood was in the air. Inside a two-by-two-metre cage, a dog and a man were fighting. The man was actually lying on the ground and being bitten by the enraged Alsatian. Some five other men were standing outside, leaning into the wire mesh with their fingers pushed through the loops. All of them were in police uniforms, in contrast to their toy for the day, who wore ragged old clothes. He might have been some homeless guy or maybe the infuriated dog had seen to his clothes. The oldest of the men, with a scarred face, which looked like it had been sewn up with the remainder of his skin like Frankenstein, was perhaps enjoying the scene in the cage most of all. He looked hypnotized, leaning on the mesh with one hand, while holding a cigarette in the other and staring. Not that he was smoking it. All he was doing was holding it in his hand, probably unable to look away from the bloodbath.

The men were so absorbed in what was going on inside the cage that they did not even notice Tomáš. Their victim lay curled up on his side and the animal was going for his weak points. Its entire maw was covered in blood and the man was trying to cover his neck. He made a fatal mistake when he hit out at its snout with his clenched fist. The dog took advantage of his uncovered weakness and bit him savagely. Blood spurted about a metre all around and the man twitched a couple of times. The scarfaced man started to urinate on the corpse and when he had finished he threw his cigarette butt at it.

Tomáš kept walking. He still felt bad. His ribs were aching, he had the feeling a hammer was pounding his temples with the same rhythm as his pulse, and he was still breathing with difficulty. He decided to go to the chapel. A group of fanatical priests had taken over for some time in the shelter. There were six of them and they could only be addressed as the 'Fathers Superior'. A bald, shrivelled priest was giving a sermon as Tomáš arrived, with hands frozen and toe joints totally numb.

The Father Superior was addressing the souls of his five congregationalists, who like Tomáš were shivering with cold.

'Jesus is with us. He was with us when Satan's henchmen first attacked. They used a new explosive, so it could be smuggled unseen into our schools and hospitals. None of us expected it. Nobody could imagine it even in their wildest dreams,' he spat spittle for metres around. 'In the name of the Devil's war they pressed the detonator button. Everybody knows what happened then – our army did the only thing it could do. It aimed our nuclear missiles at the Devil's land, at Satan's Plain, at them, all of them!' He spat angrily on the ground. 'Jesus was there with them and compassionately guided their hand, so that together they pressed the button. The hand of the Devil did not hesitate and sent down a fiery rain upon us. As it was written in the Bible, balls of fire began to fall from the heavens.' He raised his hand and looked up to the mouldy ceiling. 'And so we must live here. Like rats underground. God has renounced us and the Devil has full mastery over this world. It is with bitterness and contrition that we must now live out our lives. We had many chances to turn back, but we betrayed the Lord God. This is our punishment!'

The priest fell silent for a time and picked up a new-born baby that had some kind of disability. It had a large deformed head and shrivelled little hands. The Father Superior continued:

'Now the world is in flames and God's patience has run out, but this suffering is nothing compared to what awaits us after death!' His eyes bulged so much, they almost fell out of their sockets. 'Eternal damnation awaits us, oh Lord, because we deserve nothing else!' With these words he took a knife and cut the baby's throat. It was quite blunt, so it took some time.

After the ceremony they all left except for Tomáš, who headed for the altar. The little body lay on it motionless. Its little hands were clenched. Th pool of blood below him, which was still steaming, dripped blood onto the dirty floor. He noticed that something was moving in the corner beneath a picture of Jesus. When he examined it he saw a child, huddled under an old coat, which he pulled off to reveal, wonder of wonders, that it looked just like he did when he was about ten years old. The boy stared at him with deep eyes, stood up rapidly and embraced him. His body turned into a luminous glow, which fused with that of Tomáš, who fell to the ground, unable to breathe with sorrow. Only now did he realize why he was feeling so bad. His soul had not been with him all this time. He remembered the woman who was being raped, and his body was infused with the indescribable pain, bitterness and degradation that she went through. No, no, don't! He felt what the man in the cage went through. He felt the loss of all faith in humanity and hope. So kill me now – that was his greatest wish. What are you waiting for? He then became the disabled new-born baby.

He came into this world to make it better, to fill everything with light. He was so innocent and pure. He felt the knife at his neck, but he had no way to defend himself and he could only watch the priest's lewd face. The last thing he saw in life was his eyes, full of hate – evil in its purest form. Tomáš writhed on the ground and felt the greatest torment of his life. It had nothing at all to do with physical pain, even though he very much wished that it had. Better have all the bones in his body broken to pieces that this. He prayed for it to stop and for death. His soul was pierced by darkness. He endured the endless emptiness that is all around us, and from which he tried to escape, as if that were possible. He heard a deep horror-stricken voice:

'The darkness is coming. The world of men will fall. No one shall escape!'

At this point he woke up screaming: 'No!' His pyjamas were soaked in sweat. Eliška was sitting beside him and tousling his hair. She placed her forehead next to his perspiring brow and kept stroking him:

'Shhh, Shhh. It'll be all right. You can breathe easy. It was just another dream. I'll just go and see to Věrka.'

Perhaps he had woken her as well. Or vice versa? Eliška was standing by the cot and cradling the baby when he looked at her guiltily and said:

'I am sorry.'

She cast a loving glance at him, as only she could do, and said. 'It doesn't matter. You can't help it.'

2/20 All evil is for some good

S ummer was in full sway, the days were pleasantly warm and long, and nature had completely woken up even in the mountains. It often rained and a storm would blow past now and then. The rain cleaned and cooled pleasantly. The only defect in all this beauty was the increasing tension in society. Most people observed it uneasily, but without trying to do anything about it.

Věrka had her first illness, which was an enormous trial for her parents. Both of them breathed a huge sigh of relief when she got better. Sometimes they took her to bed with them, placed her between them and talked to her. She was rather eloquent, which they both agreed she had inherited directly from Tomáš. She often interlarded her favourite 'Heeee' with a cute 'Vaaaa', and always got them with her 'Agrrrrh'.

At the next No. 53 meeting the atmosphere was basically relaxed. At the very start, Marek bragged that he had tried out the energy approaches that Kristýna had advised for him, and he was rather enthusiastic. 'My girlfriend was totally knocked out by them.' He asked Kristýna where she knew all this from.

She gave him a crafty smile. 'I have extensive experience.'

'Extensive experience?' Jirka responded.

'Okay, I'd have told you sooner or later anyway,' and she blushed like a crayfish. The others stared at her intently. 'I used to be a nymphomaniac at one time. Ever since I was little I have longed for a strong connection with God, and in puberty I found that sex was the best way for me to achieve this. I always felt that people are as one, and I wanted to experience this to the full. Unfortunately, it came to be an addiction for me. My family were always very conservative, so except for my brother they soon all disowned me.'

A silence fell over the room. You could have heard a pin drop. Marek even stopped his munching. 'Just as well! I'd never have thought that of you, Kristýna.'

Jirka stood up for her. 'Well, I don't see any reason why you should be ashamed.'

'Ah, but I do!' Kristýna answered resolutely. 'I hurt a lot of people during that time. There were times when I even needed it three or four times a day. Of course I'm very glad I went through all that. At the time I lived very much in my heart, which was necessary. Of course, I also had to learn to think things over a little. I was very much in the clouds and needed to anchor myself.'

'It was the exact opposite with me,' Dimitri admitted. 'I was very much down to earth and I needed to release myself a little.'

'It was only later that I learnt to experience that connection without actually making love. After that I made use of my rich experience of sex for various kinds of meditation.'

'What? But how?' Marek asked in astonishment.

'Quite simply. Sex is just another form of meditation.'

Marek put his empty plate down on the table, so he could get fully involved in the discussion. 'I think people are too restrained. From an early age it's drilled into them that they should only have one sexual partner. When I started out on my sexual life, I often changed partners. There were times when I had several at the same time. At least I found out what suited me and I sowed my wild oats. Many people hold back in their youths and have problems with that later, because they have the feeling they haven't experienced anything properly. I now have broad experience and I know what suits me. What's more, I've experienced everything to the full.'

Kristýna seized on his last sentence. 'Life is too short to wait for anything. You can wait for something all your life, instead of actually living it. Go where you are drawn and don't look back. Be who you want to be, not what others want you to be. That's how I lived at the time. Mistakes are a sign of your humanity – they make you human. If we continually endeavour to go forwards we will live a meaningful life. If you live it in such a way that it is for the most part meaningful to you then people might well not understand you. They may quietly envy you, but in any case somewhere inside they will feel we were born to live life to the full and they will admire you.'

'I think it's a phase that everyone should go through in their development,' said Tomáš. 'Basically to have a period in their lives when they do what they feel like doing, regardless of what others want.'

'Have you noticed that people often find excuses for not going after what they want by saying they're concerned for others, they're working for the welfare of others and they don't have time for their own thing?' said Marek.

'It's much more intimidating to follow your own path than to do what's expected of us,' said Dimitri.

'I used to be much more selfish in the past,' said Marek. 'I had no friends. My family couldn't bear me, and now I'm glad. It taught me to not give a toss about certain things.'

'I agree, everybody has to go through this,' said Dimitri. 'The worst part of it is to look at someone you love with your whole heart and to wonder when he will grow out of it. That was the case with my son. For five long years we hardly spoke to each other. He needed to find his own way. I shall never forget what he said to me after those five years: I have found the meaning of life. To find somebody who has less of something than you and to give it to him. I have learnt to be a resource. These days I know I can help others to understand things, to show them things that only I can do and nobody else."

'That's how it was between me and my brother,' said Karla. 'No matter how much I coaxed and entreated him, he wouldn't listen. He drank a lot. He sat up at the computer well into the night. He didn't have any proper work or purpose in life. When he started taking drugs I felt I was addicted myself. Still, it did work out okay in the end. After I was put in prison my brother confided that he always knew deep down that I loved him, and now he had the opportunity to repay me.'

'After a certain period we get into a stage when our will merges with that of other people,' said Dimitri. 'We do what we love to do, and at the same time we do it as a service for society. Just as Kristýna found work in the social sphere – you can see how she finds this fulfilling, and it's clear how much she contributes to the welfare of society by doing this. Still, during our period of resistance many people become addicted in various ways.'

'Addiction to sex is like any other addiction,' said Kristýna. 'It always starts innocently enough. After the first dose you feel better and freer.

As time goes by, your yearning for this freedom actually becomes an addiction. You simply are free already. As soon as you start to think that you need something to be free then you become dependent. This is the case with ordinary drugs and with the people that you can become addicted to, as well as with sex, power and money. Fortunately, in my case it turned out okay and my addiction helped me to understand a lot of things. Above all I understand people who have ended up on the street because of their addictions. I don't feel sorry for them, because I know they themselves are responsible, but at the same time I do feel sympathy, because I went through the same thing myself.'

'The problem is that people do not go directly to God,' Dimitri said. 'They use various crutches – priests, lovers, drugs and meditation, in an effort to support their faith. But you will find God sooner where there is nothing than with some crutch. People should learn not to make God less than he is. Those crutches are only means for getting to him, which should then be discarded as soon as we become aware that we no longer need them.'

Marek could not resist. 'Crikey, this is awful. Sometimes you're as full of it as Grand Master Yoda.'

Dimitri bowed his head. 'Thank you. May the force be with you, my son.'

The room was filled with noisy laughter, but then Marek grew more serious. 'Okay, but in that case we need only go to sleep to achieve union with God. But then what if I don't seek to achieve anything by this? It just makes me happy.'

Dimitri grinned. 'That is just it! It makes you happy, which means that it connects you to yourself, replenishes your energy and flushes out the stress. The greatest masters have understood that they do not need anything just to be happy and connected. Of course, if sex, dancing, coffee drinking, mountain climbing, caring for others, stroking your cat or anything else arouses wonderful feelings in you then why the hell should you get rid of them?'

Jirka spoke up. 'A few years ago I got to be really uptight. I'd turned into a respected businessman who always insisted on correct etiquette. The small child in me died. I felt worse and worse, without realizing it. When I think back to it now, I realize I was giving less and less space to my soul. And do you know how I got out of that?' he asked, smiling broadly. 'By dancing! I found out that dancing is an unbelievable form of relaxation, whether it's at a club or at home, when I listen to Tibetan drums. Sometimes I even feel like dancing without music, and so I dance! My three-year-old son taught me to.'

'I don't think we should try to get rid of all our crutches and addictions at any cost, but we should try to free ourselves from those which are a bind,' said Tomáš. 'Simply do what fulfils us and if we don't have that then simply understand that we don't need it. Jirka's dancing has an amazing effect, and I don't think it could harm him in any way. The same goes for me with my trips to the mountains.'

'Very nicely put, Tom,' said Kristýna. 'Freedom means not having to be the person you used to be. Awareness of this was a great liberation for me. You think you need a lot of things, but you are not the person you were yesterday. And the further you get, the less you need for happiness. I felt the greatest relief when I forgave myself. People have thought up a bunch of theories and even entire religions in order to have an excuse not to forgive themselves. My behaviour has hurt a lot of people. I have to realize this and then cast off the negative feeling. Lots of people reproach themselves for things they actually put right a long time ago.'

'For me Kristýna's entire story shows just how unpredictable life can be,' said Dimitri. 'It is only after some time that we come to realize what meaning some of the events in our lives actually have. It's an amazing jigsaw puzzle. As soon as you put one picture together, you find that it's only a small part of a much larger puzzle, a much more beautiful and wonderful painting. And it is never-ending. At one time I used to often think about suicide, because there wasn't much in this world that made me happy. Everything struck me as gloomy and in-sipid. It was only years later I found this was just another stage in my life, just an interchange station.'

'Whenever the day looks too everyday, then start listening to your soul,' said Tomáš. 'You'll begin to notice the things that make life so marvellous, which cannot be seen with the eye alone.'

'And then you see life far more colourfully and you free yourself from all the stereotypes. Why should a fat man not be a good lover? Why should a woman not manage a large company? Why should old age be boring and plagued by illness?'

Marek interrupted. 'Thanks to you I have accepted one thing that I resisted for a long time. I was always afraid to put more into my heart, in case others thought I was a weakling, but during these discussions I've understood that excessive sentimentality and oversensitivity have nothing in common with being in your heart. Now I can show love and yet feel comfortable in front of others.'

'You have given us a lot too, Marek,' Dimitri said. 'As for me, you've taught me that I should never think it's all over and I've won. Because the moment you do that you are dead.'

It was already late night when Tomáš went back home. The stars glowing in the sky and the very pleasantly spent evening had put him in an excellent mood. That was exactly the way he imagined an ide-al discussion to be. People did not interrupt each other, there was no lack of fun and at the end everybody felt they had won. The atmos-phere today had reminded him of his long conversations with Kohl. That part of him that had remained in his heart had reawoken. He remembered how he had told him of the years he had spent on the street. He said that when life does not go along with our plans, we should live it to the full anyway. 'Regret as little as possible and love as much as possible,' Kohl had finished his story. As Tomáš began to recall this it all looked so clear to him. He was sure their task would work out well. And even if it didn't, people won't allow the badness in themselves to win out. There is good in everyone, even in Musílek, he considered.

Again he felt free and enjoyed the idea that he could be anything he wanted. Ever since he had joined the team, much had changed. Their relations had deepened and he had totally fallen in love with them. He understood he could love other people as well as his wife and daughter. When he compared the team's energy levels at the beginning and now, there was a considerable difference. By complementing each other they were able to generate several hundred times more energy than if they were operating on their own. In physics this is known as synergy, he recalled. The conclusions they had drawn after a couple of months only confirmed this for him. Their ideas had gradually attained increasingly higher levels and he could not wait to see what they would attain. He increasingly felt that his nightmares would not come true.

It just cannot happen. People have too much goodness in them to allow it.

2/21 A well-deserved holiday

The last meeting with the team had helped Tomáš very much to move forward and to a large extent to sort things out in his mind. He decided to come out with the truth and tell Eliška about these meetings and his dreams. In the evening, when the baby had fallen asleep, they lay down after supper and chatted. The clean bedclothes had a pleasant fragrance, and it occurred to him that this was the right moment.

'You know, Eliška, I'm really sorry, but I haven't been entirely honest with you lately.'

'I guessed you were hiding something. Have you finally found somebody like Kohl?'

'Well, he's totally irreplaceable, but it is something of that kind.'

'So stop keeping me on tenterhooks and tell me what it's about,' and she started tickling him.

'Okay, okay. I've started seeing some people who are similar to Kohl. There's five of them and we have meetings from time to time, where we deal with various matters from politics to routine matters and less routine ones, like the soul, meditation and the like.'

'Well, I'm very happy to have you. Now that we have Věrka, I've realized just what a treasure you are for me. It all actually began when you got to know Kohl. You changed, you're more attentive, kinder, wittier and far better in bed,' and she covered her mouth with her pillow. 'But then I've already told you all that. My point is that I like what you guys are talking about. It gives you the feeling that life is something wonderful and extraordinary. I'm glad you've told me. I love you.' She put the pillow back and looked candidly into his eyes.

'I love you too.'

He did not mention anything about Karla, as he presumed that would not result in such a favourable reaction. Above all he wanted his wife to feel secure.

'And why haven't you told me until now?'

'I didn't want to bother you now the baby is here, and then at first I wasn't sure what it would involve exactly. We have a certain task, so basically it's something like a working group that's trying to find a solution to the social crisis.'

'Right, well, you certainly don't do things by halves!' she said in surprise. 'Sounds to me like something from a film. I hope I'll see you protesting against human greed on TV sometime!' she burst out laughing and rolled over onto her back.

'Most of the time we chat and meditate. They really are amazing and knowledgeable about things I never imagined. When we came together, we came up with some more marvellous ideas. They also helped me with my nightmares.'

'Do you always dream the same thing?' Eliška asked, turning more serious. 'You've never answered me when I've asked. You didn't look like you wanted to talk about it. I'm glad it's better now. Last time you really frightened me.'

His throat dried up and he swallowed with difficulty. 'I have the dreams quite often these days. I didn't want them to be a worry for you.'

'And what were they previously?' she frowned a little.

He tried to describe them as simply as possible. 'It's a bit different every time, but basically I have these dreams about a future that nobody would ever want to live to see. They're full of war, pain and despair. We have to prevent that, even though we have no idea at present how to do it.'

'Prevent?' She turned back on her side. 'These are just dreams. That does actually strike me as a bit far-fetched. It would have been no problem if you'd told me straight away. I am your wife, remember?'

'Yes, I could have. At least I have now,' and he gave her a weak smile.

'But you have to promise me one thing. Discussing with friends is one thing, but getting involved in other people's lives is quite another. You could really piss people off. Promise me you won't get mixed up in anything now.'

He did not expect Eliška to fully understand what was involved, but the way she understood it now was quite enough for him. Above all he did not have to hide anything, apart from the detail that the team included an escaped prisoner convicted of manslaughter. He himself had needed some time to get used to that. It had nothing to do with whether or not she had actually done it (after all, he believed her to be innocent), but with the fact that she had been convicted, and the police were looking for her. The less his wife knew about it, the better. He kissed her.

'I promise, love. I was afraid you might tell me off. I love you.'

'Tell you off?' she chuckled. 'For going around with some people and discussing things like that? That never killed anybody. I love you.'

They started kissing and caressing each other, until, that is, the room was filled with the sound of the baby crying.

'I'll go.' He stroked Eliška's smooth face, and a heavy weight fell from his heart. He rather regretted not telling her immediately, but then he remembered what Kohl used to say. His feelings signalled that he was living a false story, so he dismissed it from his mind.

When he watched the foreign news that evening he noted that most of the conflicts had deteriorated. In Syria the army had killed three hundred demonstrators, and in Egypt large numbers of people had died in disturbances at a football stadium. One sociologist invited to the studio came out with a phrase that made quite an impression on Tomáš. 'How long can you blow a balloon up before it bursts?'

— • —

First thing in the morning Jindřiška called Tomáš into the head-mistress's study. She put a letter in front of him.

'What the hell is this meant to be?'

Reading it over quickly, he found that it was a complaint from parents about the teaching methods at the school in general, and about him in particular. He did not manage to understand exactly what he had said or done to the plaintiff's child. He read, 'Your role as a teacher is to provide information, not to tell our son how to live his life.' For a while he discussed it with the headmistress before he realized what it was about. The problem was basically that he had told Robert, the son of two respected architects, that he had to live his own life. The letter also said that Robert had put up some resistance to their expressed will, which they blamed on Tomáš.

'Damn it, Tom, do you know his parents have close ties with the mayor? You know just how much this could make it difficult for the entire school?' Jindřiška asked angrily. 'This means big trouble, un-less it's settled quickly. Call them and arrange a meeting to sort it out, okay? Apologize, say it's a misunderstanding, and tell them they are totally entitled to manage their son's life. '

'You don't actually believe that yourself, Jindřiška!' and the disenchantment could very much be heard in his voice.

'It doesn't matter what I believe. You go and sort it out. I don't want to hear any more about this.' She put her glasses on and returned to the pile of papers on her desk.

When he went over it with Eliška at home, he was quite surprised at her attitude.

'Heroism won't get you anywhere. Tell them what they want to hear. You won't change anything this way in any case.'

'It's not a question of my being heroic, but what's best for Robert.'

'Could you swear to me that your ego isn't at least playing a minor role in all of this?'

'I don't have much choice in the matter anyway. If I resist it's going to be an enormous problem, but I'm certainly not going to crawl up their backside.'

He arranged a meeting with the irate father, who sounded rather curt on the phone, for the next day. As he was mentally preparing for the meeting, he endeavoured to find out if his ego was really behind it, or if his soul had spoken to him. He was not at all sure. Whatever happens I shall make space for my soul, he thought.

When he tore into the staff room, Jan Kadlec introduced himself. It looked as if he wanted Tomáš to kiss his hand. He was perfectly groomed and wore an expensive suit. He then immediately launched into Tomáš.

'I am usually very busy, and people have to wait a month to be able to meet me, but where Robert is concerned then I will always find the time,' and he raised his head so high that Tomáš could only see two large nostrils. 'Please explain to me immediately what you had in mind. How dare you tell my son what he is to do? I hope you will clarify this for me.'

Tomáš stood stock still. He was definitely not ready for these kind of dealings. He had perhaps never seen such a large ego on anybody. It filled the entire staff room. At last he managed to say:

'Robert is a marvellous lad. You and your wife can be proud of him. I really ought to tell you how this misunderstanding came about.'

The man looked at Tomáš in a way that was clearly meant to indicate he considered him rubbish. Tomáš felt him sapping his energy.

'We are very proud of him. Other youngsters cannot hold a candle to him. So out with it.'

'In one lesson I was talking with the class about what they wanted to do in life. I take this to be one of my responsibilities within the civic studies syllabus. It was a very open discussion and the class enjoyed the lesson a lot. Robert was silent throughout, and at the end he asked me if he should speak to his parents again about his dreams. I advised him to do so.'

Robert's father turned red: 'It is your responsibility primarily to do what we pay you to do as taxpayers! Teach my boy to count and draw so he can go to college, or teach him how to behave at social events. You have no right to interfere in his upbringing, and leave your opinions about dreams for your friends in the pub!' He looked as pleased with himself as a drug addict who has just had his fix. 'Your lesson confused Robert a lot. We went over it several times with him, and he himself admitted that architecture will be much better for him in future than his football. If you want to inculcate dreams in people's heads then you get your own child. For my son you are a nobody. Nobody!'

Tomáš was seething – he felt so put down. This man had not listened to him at all. And most of what he said was not true at all! He felt like yelling everything he thought about him. And it was not very nice at all! But he did not want his pride to get him into trouble, so he took a deep breath, remembered his last meditation and connected with his soul. He knew exactly what he wanted to say and felt that it was the only right way. He looked him straight in the eye and said in a very courteous tone, 'Perhaps I am just a nobody for your son. At least I like him enough to know that his dreams have priority over my own, which can definitely not be said in your case.'

'How dare you?' he yelped at him. 'A man who is unable to do anything else except teach starts telling me what kind of a parent I am? You have finished at this school, believe me!'

He shot out of the door without closing it. Tomáš was sure he was heading straight for the headmistress's study. His feeling of self-confidence quickly evaporated as he began to consider the consequences of what he had just done. A couple of minutes later the telephone rang.

'Come to my study right now!'

He knew very well that another unpleasant conversation awaited him, so he set off immediately. The longer he left her waiting the worse it would be. He could feel his heart pounding. When he entered the headmistress's study, Jindřiška was sitting on her desk and smoking. He had only seen her like that twice in his life before, and he very quickly understood that he was in deep trouble.

'You don't give me any other option, Tom. To protect the school I have had to promise Mr Kadlec that I am releasing you. Now go home. You are on leave until the end of the week. Come in on Monday, and we shall talk about what happens next.'

He was going to say something, as if there were an answer to that, but he judged by her expression that he'd better quickly up and leave.

When he got to the staff room he began to pack his things. Honza presently appeared at the door and gaped. 'What's going on, Tom?! Petr and Marek told me that Jindřiška wants to sack you.'

He could not resist a wry comment. 'News like that spreads like wildfire, doesn't it?' And he quickly described what had happened.

'Have you gone mad, Tom? Good God! What are you going to do now? I can't believe Jindřiška would fire you just like that. Not after all you've done for the school.'

'It's not for sure yet,' he lowered his gaze. 'I'll know for sure on Monday. I'm on leave till the end of the week, so keep your fingers crossed,' and he disappeared through the door. On the way from the staff room he bumped into Karel. He'll be all geed up about giving me a good going over now, he thought, expecting the worst. This was right up his street. Both of them stopped, but Karel had an expression of approval on his face.

'I've heard what you've done. I have to admit you surprised me. I thought you were just a regular sissy, but now I see you've got balls.'

He was so surprised that he did not even manage to answer. As he got nearer to home he felt worse and worse. A few metres from his block it would have been hard to call what he was going through a bad mood. He felt like he was right back at square one. And he was furious like never before.

How am I going to tell Eliška? he wondered. It was difficult to find a new job with the economic crisis on, and he had taken such a risk! More and more people were out of work, and he might well soon join their ranks. How could he have been so irresponsible? Clearly, he had made a mistake when he'd listened to his soul, which had brought about some fine problems! If only Kohl were here...

He now finally fully understood the frustrations of ordinary people. The uncertainty totally overwhelmed them. He did not know if he would have enough money to feed his family. It's easy to be positive when you have the money to pay the bills. It's easy to be calm and listen to your soul. It's easy to meditate, but what if you don't know if you will have enough for food and clothing for your child next month? If you cannot be sure your family will not be robbed in the street?

In this state of mind the debates at No. 53 seemed pointless and totally removed from reality, except for one aspect, which was unfortunately very important. It now made total sense to him that people would trust and follow anybody who would give them back their security, even somebody like Musílek, rather than leave their family without funds. It had been so naive of him to patronize Robert's father. He had been so naive to think he could change the world! At last he had sobered up.

When he got home Eliška was feeding the baby. He wanted to tell her when she had finished, but she was not to be put off and kept on asking. Little Věrka was happily drinking, but Eliška became sadder and sadder as it sank in just what had happened at school. She remained silent, quietly put the baby in the cot, and then answered. 'What are we going to do when they sack you? That boy is none of your business. You swallow your pride and tell them at school that you're sorry, and next time you'll make sure you don't lead the children astray again, please!' she insisted.

'If it isn't already too late.'

'At least give it a try. We have to look after the baby,'

Of course he agreed. Indeed he had expected Eliška to be totally incensed, but she took it all quite well. At least one of us is mature and responsible, he thought, recalling the way Kohl had described a loving relationship: 'It is always led by the one who has the best connection, the highest intuition, basically more energy.'

They did not speak much more for the rest of the evening, as the apartment was steeped in a gloomy mood. Around seven he received a text message that an extraordinary meeting had been hurriedly convened, and that he was to be at No. 53 within an hour. He hesitated for a while, but his curiosity eventually got the better of him. His wife did not take it very well.

'Do what you want to!'

2/22 The argument

On the way to the meeting Tomáš's unquiet mind was assailed by one thought after another, but he did not remain with any single one for too long: Why has the meeting been called so hurriedly? This has never happened before. What happened at school? How will it all turn out? What did I actually dream about in that nightmare when I lost my soul? What was it supposed to tell me? When I was talking to Matěj, it was all very clear to me. Why isn't it now?

Is it better to tell the truth or to keep your mouth shut and stay in line?

Wasn't I naive when I thought I could listen to my soul without any serious consequences?

He was angry with himself.

Where has that carefree Tomáš gone?

What has happened to me?

He came to a long halt over this thought, and try as he might, he could not come up with an adequate answer. Sullen, he arrived at No. 53, where they were now only waiting for Jirka, who had an important appointment outside town. This meeting had been called because of Marek, who had some important information regarding Musílek.

Kristýna did not need much time to notice that something was wrong with Tomáš. He poured it all out, and the others were taken aback, as if their friend, whom they had been regularly seeing for the past six months, was not at all the man they had thought him to be. He finished his story: 'I was naive.'

Kristýna stroked his hand. 'I wouldn't call that naivety, but love. I think this is the right time for meditation.'

This idea did not appeal to him at all, but he nodded.

A couple of minutes later the living room was full of lit candles and they were sitting in a circle with eyes closed, breathing deeply. Kristýna started talking. 'You are standing on the edge of a deep abyss, surrounded by the unknown. You have nowhere further to go. Doom is raining down upon you and chills run down the back of your neck. Your feet are burning with the frost, your knees are shaking, and your heart is beating with its final strength. Slower and slower. All around there is nothing but empty, lifeless desert. You are hungry and you feel incredibly alone. There is nothing here to sustain you. You fall into the void, and there is nobody to catch you. You see nothing but darkness and despair. Several times you feel a faint quiver of hope and you put all your effort into standing up again. With your last strength you manage to, only to fall back down again. Somewhere inside you feel you are not going to get up again. You remain lying, in endless emptiness and oblivion, which will remain forever unperceived. Remember well this endless despair and hopelessness and the freezing void that you are now experiencing. Remember it well, and now let it go. Let it go. Let it go. Let it go! Only you remain. Pure love and endless wisdom. A brilliant, incandescent sun in the middle of a freezing, desolate universe. Your rays reach out to all its corners. Sometimes it takes thousands of years for them to penetrate even those darkest places, but eventually they will get there. It is enough to keep shining and to just let it be.'

Tomáš felt warm all over and fell into a deep state of meditation. When he came to, Jirka had arrived. All the others were also awoken. Kristýna examined him, and the corners of her mouth slowly lifted:

'That's how I like it. How are you feeling?'

'Like the sun,' and he stretched and realized he had not smiled at all in recent days.

Marek could no longer wait, however: 'We waited for you to come round. I have some important info. For several weeks now I have been running through secret police records and trying to find some evidence against Musílek. Now I can tell you that what I was talking about last time is only the tip of the iceberg.'

He brought out a laptop from his bag and continued. 'There are dozens of strange disappearances, sudden deaths and people behind bars, who evidently should not be there.'

Jirka exhaled out loud: 'This is rather more serious than we thought. And have you found any proof, or is this all just suspicion?'

'If you'd let me speak then I'd tell you straight away.' He was enormously pleased at having all the attention now. For a while he tapped something into his computer as if he were looking for something. 'I've found something better than proof. While you have been looking for ways to persuade people to listen to their souls, I have found a witness who will help us get rid of Musílek!'

He waited some time for the sake of dramatic effect, and then added in amusement, 'You should have seen your expressions just then! This guy I found is Musílek's former colleague Chrobák. He was supposed to have died in a car crash somewhere abroad, but I have found him alive and well. Unless corpses can smoke cigars, that is. And best of all, I don't think Musílek has even guessed he's still alive. By all indications he has some important evidence against Musílek, and that is why he had to disappear.'

'That sounds good. We have to contact him,' Dimitri said with some caution.

'I even have his residential address. It's in Kenya.'

Jirka did not stint on praise. 'Hats off, Marek. I can arrange the air tickets for you, though I won't be able to go with you.'

Several separate conversations now broke out in the room, as everybody wanted to say something. Dimitri had to calm them down:

'Settle down please! Before any of us fly off there, one thing needs to be said very clearly.' Presently they stopped shouting over each other. 'This is really starting to get very risky for all of us. It looks like Musílek does not hesitate to kill anybody who gets in his way. If anything goes wrong then it could end up very badly. We all have the opportunity to back out now. Whatever you decide, the others will certainly understand, because we are doing this voluntarily. Only after that are we to talk about a trip to Kenya.'

'Well, I'm in,' said Marek resolutely. Dimitri also confirmed his participation, as did Kristýna, Tomáš and Jirka in turn. The last one was Karla, who hesitated a little, but eventually nodded.

They agreed that Tomáš, Karla, Marek and Kristýna would fly off to Kenya to persuade Chrobák to help them. Jirka arranged the permits, visas and other requisites for them.

— • —

Tomáš came back home late that evening. He immediately started packing his things for his trip to Kenya the following day. He still couldn't believe it – risking his own security and that of his family for a plan that was not bound to work at all. However, somewhere deep inside he felt he had to go. He wondered what he would say to Eliška in the morning. Or should he leave a note on the table to explain everything? He probably could not just leave without saying good-bye. What if he did not come back? Before he managed to think it through, his dilemma was resolved for him. She was standing opposite him in the doorway with raised eyebrows and arms akimbo.

'What are you doing then?'

'I have to tell you something. Come and sit with me here at the table, will you?' He dropped his rucksack with the things he had prepared, and took her by the hand.

'You know, I haven't been totally honest with you. The people I've been meeting with have found out that the former Police Commissioner, who's responsible for extortion, several frauds and even murders, wants to get into power. We have to stop him. We have to convince a crown witness to testify against him.' He swallowed with difficulty, and she just sat there motionless like a waxworks figure at a museum exhibition, until she eventually came round.

'I just don't understand. What is this about? Why you? Where are you going?'

'If Musílek gets into power then in all probability he is going to create a police state. He'll want unlimited power. And the team won't get by without me. Please believe me when I say I've thought it over a few times and I have to do it. I'm not going to allow this murderer, extortionist and fraudster to get into power.'

Eliška straightened up and thrust away his hand. 'What the hell have you got into? Is this some kind of conspiracy theory? The ex-Commissioner isn't a murderer. It's just totally unreal that anybody's going to create a dictatorship. God almighty, get a grip, Tom!'

'But it is for real, Eliška. Believe me! You have no idea the threat we are under,' and he tried to explain it to her, but without any great success.

'You have a wife and a child! That's reality! Why do you have to go making things up? Is ordinary life not good enough for you? I really did not expect this of you.' She stood up angrily from the table, knocking everything off it. She had no desire to go into it any further.

'That's not the point. You know I love you and Věrka. At first it looked innocent, but then it all got confused and now we're in a situation where we have to step in. Please believe me this is no fantasy.'

'Why are you doing this? Darling, just look at yourself. You're living in a different world. A world where police commissioners are murderers, where a dictator is nearly in power. But if you think about it just a little at least, you'll find it's complete nonsense. Why do you have to be so selfish?' she shouted.

He stood up as they were now both shouting: 'I just didn't want to lie to you. Is that so selfish?!'

Wordlessly she went into the bedroom. The thought passed through his mind: What if she's right? And this time he was the one who felt like a waxworks figure. What if their meetings to save the world were just their little distraction from boring, everyday life? What if they had been embellishing reality for so long that they had landed in a completely different world? What if everything he had believed all this time was just a lie?

The only way to find out for sure was to fly off now to see Chrobák in Kenya. If they found him and he confirmed what the others had said then it was true. If they did not find him, or if he said something else, then it was all made up.

He decided to tell her this. She was standing over the cot and wiping her red face. He managed to stammer:

'Y-You are right. I might well have been living an illusion all this time. I have to find out! I have to fly and find out for myself.'

'You've let me down. Get away from me!'

He finished getting his things together and lay down on the living room sofa. In all the time they had been together he had only ever had to resort to this twice. Now he was 'enjoying' it for the third time. He was very sorry. If he had been living an illusion then this behaviour would hardly excuse it.

In the morning he met up with Karla, Marek and Kristýna, and they went to the airport together. The boarding passes were ready for them at the flight desk as Jirka had promised. Marek had prepared a map and directions to get to Chrobák. Kristýna noticed that Tomáš was a little fretful and tried to get him to say what the matter was. He did not have the least desire to talk about it, so he put her off by saying that he had had an argument at home with his wife and that he did not want to talk about it. He was glad that he did not have to lie. The others respected this and discussed various things to do with the journey that day. The flight to Kenya was to last about six hours. He did not even know what city they would be landing in or where they were to look for Chrobák. Nor was he particularly interested. He was tired, as he had not slept very much that night. As soon as he sat down in his seat, his eyes began to droop.

Part three: The Choice

3/23 Between two worlds

Hands and feet numb with cold, he woke up for a moment, wrapped himself up in his blanket and went back to sleep again, only to be reawoken by an unpleasant, high-pitched sound. It was the alarm. He started coughing, his head was swimming and he breathed with difficulty. He felt drunk and could not think clearly. A moment later he realized what was happening. Others around him had started to wake up and someone behind him shouted:

'Fire! What are we going to do?'

He got out of bed, but was so feeble that he was barely able to stay on his feet. There was smoke everywhere, and he could hardly see a metre in front of him. He started running towards where he thought the exit was. He was scared to death when he tripped up and fell with a crash. He could not get up and had probably broken a leg. His ribs were also quite bruised, so he moaned every time he tried to catch his breath. This is the end – I'm going to die here, and he gave way to despair and came to terms with it. A few moments later his mind became more alert as he realized he was breathing better and could even see a little. The light came from somewhere to his right. He turned in that direction and tried to get there as fast as possible on all fours, having to go round some beds on the way. From some of them drooped the hands of people who had not managed to wake up. Others yelled, coughed and pleaded for help. Nearby somebody fell.

There was confusion everywhere, and he could barely stand the cries of choking people. His eyes misted over, but eventually he began to recognize the outlines of the main complex doors. He gasped with his last strength. When he realized that the gates were slowly closing, his heart exploded as never before. Through his peripheral vision he saw a burning human body that was convulsively throwing itself around trying to put itself out. Rapidly casting this scene from his mind, he tried to reach safety. He would not manage to do that on all fours! He held his breath, painfully got to his feet and ran towards the doors. With every stride on his injured leg a sharp pain pierced his spine. Everything went black, but he leapt towards the place he had seen the door. It was all the same to him whether it was open or not.

His head hit something hard and he fell headlong. He did not know if he had managed to get out, as his vision was still blurred, his head was going round, he was unable to maintain his attention and he could not breathe properly. He had not made it!

Somebody helped him up: 'Follow me!' The only thing he managed to identify was the reflective stripes on a police uniform sleeve. He was taken into a room of some kind and ordered, 'Sit down here and don't move.'

He had no idea how long it had taken him to come round. There were other people there together with him. Some of them had frightened, vacant expressions, while others were quietly talking. A couple of injured people were there too. A young dark-haired man was sitting beside him:

'Hey, my name's Pavel. What's yours?'

Befuddled, Tomáš answered and gave him a good looking-over. Pavel was around ten years younger with boyish features. He spoke extremely fast, slightly mispronouncing his r's.

'I've heard they're cleaning out one part of the poor block, so they have somewhere to put us.'

Tomáš knew very well what they meant by cleaning out, but it was all the same to him. The main thing was that he would have somewhere to live. They chatted on for a while. Then Pavel started to whisper, 'We won't last longer than a year in the shelter. Just look round. Thanks to the floods and the cave-ins the space in the shelter is getting smaller and smaller. And then this fire. We're running out of food and water. Outside it's safe, but here they have us under control. They told us all that we'd die up above just to keep us in their power.'

'Hey, you can't talk like that here. What if somebody heard you? Have you gone mad?' And he hushed him.

'I don't care. Do you want to escape with me?'

'It's too late. It was already too late for us when the first bomb fell.'

'How do you mean?'

'Just as I say. We brought it on ourselves. We thought we could do whatever we felt like. We lived under the illusion that we'd rule the whole world. And we didn't even manage to stop our own species from destroying itself.'

Pavel just stared at him uncomprehendingly. Tomáš opened his mouth, but he wasn't thinking about what he was saying at all, as if in a trance. 'We were banging our heads against a brick wall and we did not want to see it. We supported each other in believing that we could live that way without any consequences. It only struck a few people as strange that the most affluent countries in the world were investing hundreds of billions in the armaments industry and leaving millions of people to die of hunger and common diseases. Even fewer people found it unjust and openly criticized it. Instead of helping each other we exerted all our energy on having the best and most efficient weapons to kill each other with, ha! And we all said it was the only way to maintain peace. Can you imagine? Such stupidity!' And he palmed his face. 'Were your family in Prague when it happened?'

'I was actually visiting my parents in Vienna when it all began. Our daughter was ill, so my wife stayed with her at home in Prague.' As he spoke the youth in his voice evaporated.

'I am sorry.'

'When I found out I wanted to take a gun and shoot all the slant-eyed bastards I met. I took part in the first pogroms against them. We killed some and beat up others, dragged them off to a ship and told them to go and never come back. When the war began I joined the army, but our leaders are no better than those of the enemy, so I joined the central shelter staff. I manage the ration system here. What about you?'

The people around were totally ignoring their conversation, or were at least pretending to. Tomáš inspected his injured leg and his voice reflected the apathy that he felt: 'I'm a teacher, a healthy, fertile man and what's more, I do as they say, so they found a job for me. My family are probably dead. I often think I should have died along with them.'

Pavel nodded and Tomáš saw in his eyes that he wished for the same thing. He stared at the ground and said, 'You escape without me. I don't have anything to live for anyway.'

A police officer appeared in the doorway and handed out bags of clean clothes for everybody. Then they were taken off towards the poor block, where it was dreadfully cold and he was only wearing pyjamas. The fire had probably knocked out the heating system. One part of the wall was blackened by smoke.

On the way he noticed the plaster on the connecting tunnel corridors was flaking, and in some places the wall was partially breached with metal wires hanging out from it. Here and there water seeped through the ceiling and leaked down: drip... drip... drip. Elsewhere the ceiling had partially caved in and the floor was strewn with rubble.

When they got to their new home they were presented with a charming sight. The air stank of faeces that was probably not far away. Water dripped down the walls, which were all mouldy. One of the corridors had caved in, so there was only one way in and out. There were just some wires hanging out where a bulb should have been, so the lighting was provided by a couple of halogen lamps on extensions. He lay down on his bed with just one thought passing through his mind: The end is nigh. He was so tired that he fell asleep immediately.

He woke up in the airplane, and for the next ten minutes sat and stared ahead. He did not know if he had just awoken from a dream or not. For a long time he wondered if this was reality. Kristýna looked at him and did not say anything. She guessed he had had one of his dreams. After a while the others asked him what the matter was.

'Those dreams again,' he snapped, rueful that he was unable to clearly tell the difference between dream and reality, but gradually things started to come into focus, like a film photograph being developed. What he had just been through was a dream and the airplane was the reality.

After another hour of flight they got off in Nairobi. Everything was trouble-free until they got to passport control. It seemed the airport security had some problems with Karla's passport. Kristýna discreetly caught Tomáš and Marek by the hand and whispered:

'You remember our last meditation?' The next moment the police officer handed back Karla's passport and wished her a pleasant holiday in broken English.

They exchanged their euros for Kenyan shillings and hired a car. Tomáš felt uncomfortable at the driving wheel – he was not used to driving on the left, but he got into it after about twenty minutes. Marek gave him instructions.

'Now turn left here and get onto the motorway to Mombasa. We need to get to the Amboseli National Park.'

Meanwhile the girls in the back seat were talking about what had happened at passport control. Kristýna explained to Karla that a quick meditation had cleaned them up and got rid of all the fears they were sending in her direction. The police officer then did not have anything to pick up off them and let her go.

Karla could not conceal her enthusiasm: 'You are marvellous, Kristýna!'

Kristýna in turn stroked Karla's hair. 'Every individual has the power to take something ugly and turn it into something wonderful.'

The motorway looked good. It was modern and driving along it was easy. The same could definitely not be said of the other Kenyan roads. Ultimately Tomáš was glad that Karla had had the last word on hiring a car, and they had taken the largest SUV that they had at the car hire centre. After travelling for an hour along the worst road they could imagine, they came to a barrier. It was the official entrance to the park. The men guarding the barrier did not want to entertain the idea of letting in their car, but eventually let themselves be bribed. Tomáš commented, 'I'm glad some things here work just like in our country.'

When they presently spotted a couple of giraffes it was quite an experience for him. Marek gave them some basic information as they were coming near to their destination. 'He's divorced from his wife. Both his parents died of cancer. He has a daughter and a son. Both of them have stayed in the Czech Republic and are studying at university.'

Tomáš was a little shocked at all the personal information that could be found out about an individual. After twenty minutes on an even bumpier and muddier road, they came to a small village.

'That building!' Marek pointed to one of the largest and best-looking houses in the neighbourhood, where a man was sitting out on the veranda and smoking a cigar.

His appearance reminded Tomáš of Kohl. He puffed away in satisfaction and when he saw them he commented, 'I always wanted to go on safari. The people are very pleasant, the countryside is marvellous and it isn't as bloody cold as it is at home.'

Marek spoke up. 'I left a message with your intermediary, so you'll know why we are here. My name is Marek, and these are Tomáš, Karla and Kristýna.'

'So this is the famous Karla! This young lady taught me one thing. That even in this fucked-up world there are still people with morals. And they all end up the same way.'

She stared into his wrinkled eyes: 'That's not what we are here for. That is all behind me. We need your help. We both know what Musílek is all about, right, Mr Chrobák?'

'Call me Miloš, dear. But then why should I help you?'

Kristýna exerted a large amount of energy to persuade Miloš. 'Because even though you are living here, it cannot be all the same to you what is happening at home. You are not indifferent to what is happening to the world. What is happening in our country is just the start, Miloš. If you help us there is hope that the good in us will eventually win out. For that reason alone we should not give up.'

But her words did not fall on fertile soil. 'Young lady, it is now all the same to me what kind of world I live in. I don't have long. I came here to live out my unaccomplished life. Or to be more precise, I don't give a damn what happens to this bloody world! People are to blame for it themselves. Now clear off! If you step on it, you'll get back to the airport while it's still light.'

If nothing else then at least this convinced Tomáš that it wasn't all fiction. It was true that Musílek planned to take over the Czech Republic and purge those who did not agree with him. God knows how. He chose different tactics to Kristýna's: 'You knew we were coming and yet you stayed, which means it isn't all the same to you. You can sit in that rocking chair and watch as your child's carefree youth comes to an end. You can sit and watch as somebody starts to dictate to him what he is to study and how he is to live. You might even live long enough to see them put your children into the Hitlerjugend. Or you can get off your backside and do something about it. Self-pity doesn't suit you. You used to be a highly regarded, upstanding man and you can be one again. If we are successful, you can see your family again. It is not too late.'

Miloš got up from his rocking chair, stubbed out his cigar and growled: 'For me it is.'

Kristýna called after him. 'Wait!'

He stopped for a moment with his back turned towards them.

'Here's an air ticket for you. The plane leaves at six this evening. If you change your mind.' And she placed it on the old wooden table. As they watched his receding figure, Marek commented resignedly, 'Well there we go, we ought to be off.'

The others nodded and got into the car. On the way back they did not speak very much, until Kristýna said, 'Stop here please, Tom. This is an excellent place for meditation.'

They parked by the side of the road. It was a truly magnificent place. Sturdy trees rose sky-high and provided shelter against the fierce noonday sun. There were only a few dozen of them on the enormous plain, and they were always quite far apart from each other. The grass was golden and the air was pleasantly fresh. Kristýna led them under the largest tree around, which looked truly ancient and very well-preserved. They sat in a circle and the meditation was led as always by Kristýna. This time she did not speak very much.

Tomáš soon became drowsy as he noticed the countryside around him. He felt he was a tree. For a while he then became the grass and all the little creatures living in it. Eventually he fell asleep completely. When he woke up the others were in conversation. Kristýna was saying, 'The only thing we can do is to send Miloš energy. He might still change his mind. Still, the decision is his and we cannot coerce him into anything. In any case I am sure we will accomplish the task without him.'

As soon as they had been through check-in, they waited in a hall to be let onto the plane. An hour before the flight a foreigner with a little suitcase appeared beside them. At first they did not recognize him. Miloš had changed into a jacket and was wearing a hat. Before they managed to react, he said, 'You've got balls. I have to give you that. But without me you are definitely going to screw up. Now how did you find me anyway?'

Marek answered with considerable self-satisfaction, 'You smoke a very fine brand of cigar, but unfortunately you are the only one in Africa to do so. Your cigar consignments were sent to you with absolute regularity.'

Miloš cooled their ardour a little. 'But don't go thinking I believe you're going to stop Musílek. I don't have much time left. I'm going to die of cancer soon, so let's try to make sure it's not in vain.'

'I am sorry,' Karla said sympathetically.

But Miloš was not concerned: 'I don't need any pity. What's your plan anyway?'

'We're going to hide you at my place and press charges against Musílek.'

Miloš looked around to see if anybody was listening. 'That's the biggest load of nonsense I have ever heard. It won't work like that. I'll be dead before you've even filed a criminal complaint. I know this police officer – one of the few who still has principles, who I can trust. Get me to him and he'll look after my security. With his help I'll also sort out a way to charge Musílek.' When he had finished speaking he lifted up his little case and tapped it.

'But how can we trust you?' Marek asked what the others wanted to know too.

He bared his yellowed teeth: 'You can't. You have no power over me or any way of enforcing it.'

Kristýna gazed into his eyes lovingly: 'We trust you.' Then Marek gave him a passport with a false name and an identity card with the same details.

As soon as Miloš had inspected them, he gave him a measured stare:

'As a former police officer, I have to admit this is a masterpiece. Indistinguishable from an original. You've hacked into the police and post office systems, and you have access to forged documents like that. I admit I am impressed, and just a decade ago I'd have had you put away for keeps!'

It was on the flight that Karla finally had the opportunity to ask him, 'So what went on between you and Musílek then?'

Again he checked to see if anybody was listening. Then he whispered, 'At first we were best of friends. Musílek was always a dreamer – he wanted to change the world. Then it happened with his wife. She was unfaithful and eventually left him. For a long time he couldn't deal with it. It completely broke him. Ever since he's been a different man. He started suspecting lots of people around him of wanting to harm him. He didn't trust anybody at all. He always wanted to have total control of the situation. He wouldn't let anyone get the edge over him.'

'So it's his wife who's responsible for everything?' Marek chipped in, and Miloš looked daggers at him.

Kristýna answered, 'No, that was just the trigger. He must have had it inside him all along. You can harm people as much as you like, but if they haven't had tendencies like that since they were small then it's hard to bring them out.'

'And what happened then? Why did you escape?' Karla asked.

'I found out that Musílek was behind some strange disappearances or unexplained murders. Some of the traces led directly to him. He might not have trusted anybody, but he was not always entirely on his guard against his best friend. I wanted to know the truth, so I told him. He answered that I was being absurd, but I knew him like the back of my hand. Whenever he lied he used to rub his hands unawares. If he had managed to murder or get rid of inconvenient people, many of whom were his friends, he would not have had a problem dealing with me too. I escaped and stage managed my own death, so he wouldn't come looking for me, and to make sure he left my family alone.'

Tomáš took advantage of the long flight to think all this over. He kept trying to find some discrepancy in what had gone on that day. A discrepancy to prove it was all some illusion. But it all turned out to make sense and be logical. He asked his soul what he was to do.

It is all an illusion. Hold on to what seems right to you.

3/24 Electoral system

He must have slept for a long time. When Tomáš awoke it was already late in the morning. Still half-asleep he walked out of the bedroom, but what he saw woke him up straight away. Eliška was sitting motionless with mouth agape in front of the television set, holding the baby in her arms.

'What's happened?' he cried out in alarm.

She came to herself a couple of moments later. 'Mu-Musílek has set up a political party. It looks like some deputies have joined him.'

Shaking his head, he watched the live transmission from the studio alongside her. 'I just don't understand this.'

He heard the phone ringing from the bedroom. It was Kristýna. She asked him to come over immediately. He was able to get there in the car in a couple of minutes. On the way his uneasy mind was trying to work out what Musílek was up to. He had a strange gnawing sensation in the pit of his stomach and felt so preoccupied that he had to be very careful he kept to the traffic regulations. An angry driver had beeped him just now as Tomáš cut him up. He ran up the stairs and it was Kristýna who answered the door, looking good as always: 'Pleased to see you.'

Everyone in the room had the same perplexed expression as Dimitri addressed them. 'I don't know how he has managed to get all those politicians into his party. In theory he could gain a majority in parliament and do whatever he wanted, but he cannot possibly succeed! He would have to persuade a lot more of them.'

Marek palmed his face. 'Damn! Why didn't I realize earlier?' and five pairs of eyes were glued onto him. 'The point is, when Musílek was in the police he had plenty of time to dig up important information on these politicians. From banal things, like when and where they broke the speed limit or were fined for disorderly conduct to serious matters like suspicion of corruption or whether or not they received their university degree in a fair way. He even knows if any of them have a lover or socialize with the wrong people, or if their children have any problems. I had it under my nose all the time! I suspected that he was getting too much information, but eventually I just let it be.'

Karla could not conceal her dismay. 'Good God! I can't believe it!'

Tomáš put two and two together: 'Of course, this means he must have some dirt on most of our politicians, but surely he can't get away with that.'

'What are we going to do?' asked Kristýna, the calmest of them all.

'Above all we have to hope that Mr Chrobák does not have second thoughts. We can also publicize it all – come out with everything we know,' said Jirka.

'Jirka's right,' said Dimitri. 'We have to make it public. If he gets into power now then he'll immediately start to consolidate. We cannot allow him to do that!' He clenched his fists, but relaxed again straight away. 'We have never spoken about it here, but I think now is the best time. For a long time I have studied the human brain, motivation and decision-making. Sit down and I shall explain it for you.'

When they had calmed down a little, and Jirka had stopped nervously pacing up and down, Dimitri began. 'Basically, our minds are all connected. The closer two people are to each other, the more they are connected up to each other. Thanks to the mass media the majority of people now know about Musílek, and they are subconsciously connecting up to him. Some people will want him to get into power, while others will not. Whether or not they talk about it, they will make a decision in their minds – they will make a choice. They have two choices, yes or no. How they decide depends on dozens, possibly hundreds of variables.'

Jirka saw where he was leading and backed him up. 'From the psychological perspective, the people who see the future bleakly will decide for Musílek. They'll automatically vote for him, as they'll want a strong leader in power to look after them even at the price of losing their freedom.'

'Like a new form of slavery,' interrupted Tomáš. 'On the other hand those who have greater trust in the world, and those who believe in themselves, will vote against Musílek in any conceivable elections.'

'Our souls are basically one,' said Dimitri. 'They have a single will. In simple terms we might say that this single soul wants the best for all of us. However, this will then develops into the specific wishes of individual people or of their souls. Hence two similar people in the same situation may react completely differently. Nobody knows the overall plan. In my many years of research I have also come up against another issue. Each choice is based not just on what it provides you, but also on how important the decision is. Otherwise you would be making decisions on what you have for lunch before you decide who to marry. If we knew that a particular choice provided particular results then we would automatically choose the option that best matches the overall plan. The one that makes us happier.'

Jirka hit the nail on the head. 'This is the problem with most people. Their souls want something that their minds consider to be total nonsense. Something that could cause them pain, but then the soul sees the overall plan. If we follow this then we're bound to be happy over the long term.'

Now Tomáš remembered what had happened to him at school and that he was under the threat of the sack. It all started to make more sense. His soul had a plan! He said, 'You are right, so the only choice is whether or not to keep to the overall plan or not.'

Kristýna attempted to explain all this. 'It's not that you have to listen to something you disagree with. What you want is what your soul wants and vice versa. What's more, the overall plan is not unchangeable. As we grow and develop, it develops too. It is difficult to speak about it. These are things that the mind will never understand.'

Dimitri carried on from where she had left off. 'So it doesn't mean you've lost control over your life, when you decide to act within the framework of the overall plan. All our lives we seek something that will fulfil the longings of our ego and our soul, and that is only right. We're constantly developing and changing. You can actually do whatever you want, and if it goes against the overall plan then the soul will let you know. You'll be given this little kick.' Tomáš found this now made sense.

'But how do I tell the "important" choices from the "unimportant" ones? It is often the trivial things, like should I get into this car or not? that can have a fundamental influence on your life.'

Tomáš knew the answer to this. 'Your entire life revolves around the little decisions. These sometimes influence your life more than the big ones. We are constantly transmitting our choices all around us. Our choices always have an effect on other people's decision-making. Hence choice is as important as the number of people it ultimately influences. If you get into a car and you cause an accident that affects the lives of five people, that is an important choice.'

Marek added, 'It actually affects the lives of far more people. Each of them has their own family and friends. Surely you know the butterfly effect.'

Karla also began to follow. 'Aha, so that is why some decisions are so important and others are not. If you decide on something that will affect you for the rest of your life, then logically it will affect hundreds of other people – all those you meet throughout your life.'

'And the decision on Musílek will initially affect ten million people, because that will be a huge change in the style of state government. It's hard to imagine anybody not being affected by living in a police state.'

Marek went even further. 'And that in its turn will affect hundreds of millions of Europeans.'

Now Dimitri raised another associated point. 'At the moment you decide, you put your vote in the ballot box. Everybody decides for themselves, either consciously or unconsciously. Because we live in a constantly changing world, we can think our choice over. It all depends on what we experience, who we meet and how we actually feel. We can change our mind until the key moment arrives. Then our choice is set in stone, and we can no longer take it back. After that we can make a different choice, perhaps the complete opposite, but the initial choice has been made and will bring us a particular set of consequences.'

Marek simplified his description a little. 'If we imagine the state to be like a processor, then at a precisely given moment people are divided into zeros and ones. It is at this moment that each person sends his preference.'

Dimitri attempted to summarize the entire discussion: 'Every choice that has been set in stone has its invariable consequences. Out of the thousands of choices that we make every day, we have to focus on the "weight-bearing" ones, that is the choices whose consequences change our lives for better or worse over the long term and thus in turn affect hundreds of people for better or worse. What is amazing about life is that you never know just how important a particular choice will be: belting up in the car, going down a particular street that evening or meeting a particular person. We often only realize later how important a particular choice was.'

Tomáš gave a specific example. 'Like the time I was deciding whether or not to listen to Naďa, when she contacted me and said I should meet you. I didn't attach any importance to it, and now it seems to have been one of the most important decisions in my life.' The others agreed they saw this in a similar way.

Kristýna reminded everybody: 'Each choice is automatically correct if you listen to your intuition.'

Then Jirka revealed the secret of his success. 'So when you focus on the important decisions and you decide "correctly", you need not make any effort at all in life and you'll be happy. That is why some people are more successful. They focus on the essential choices and they decide correctly at the important moment.'

Karla came up with a very good question. 'What role does money play?'

'Money is the index of your power,' Marek said. 'The more you have, the more you can influence what others will choose, whether you pay them directly or indirectly.'

'For example, with a subliminal advertisement,' Jirka smiled.

Kristýna had found a loophole in this theory, however. 'But this does not always apply. Some people have the power to influence others' choices even though they don't have much money. Where does their power come from?'

Dimitri knew how some acquire power without money. 'Because people have identified with them – they act as their models. For some reason people admire them and take them as their authority. If somebody like that does something, people automatically consider their decision to be a model for their own decision-making.'

Jirka knew very well what the advertisement was based on that said, 'You don't need to be a model and you don't need to have money, and yet you can influence what people choose. All you need to know is how people's minds work – what they are afraid of and what they love.'

'Just like Musílek,' said Karla.

Jirka had come up with something that could help: 'Going public might not be enough. Nor can we rely on Miloš providing that testimony. We need some insurance – what if we spoke with the Prime

Minister and warned him about this? I can get access to him for us.'

Dimitri nodded. 'He has considerable powers. For example, he could press for early elections. That would at least complicate life for Musílek. After all, winning elections is only a little more difficult than blackmailing politicians,' he smiled. 'It's been a great discussion. Even though I've wondered about the ways people vote for several years, it's only today that I've fully understood. Thank you all. When can you get us to see the Prime Minister, Jirka?'

3/25 Prime Minister

When Tomáš got home he told Eliška everything they had been talking about that day. They argued like never before. He tried to remain calm, but only succeeded to some extent. Eliška went completely overboard, threatening to move out and divorce, shouting: 'come back down to earth! You have a family! You have your obligations.' But this did nothing to change his mind.

A silence ensued. Tomáš felt as if a tornado had torn through, not sparing anything, even if their heated argument left no actual traces on the apartment furniture. Eliška meant a lot to him, but she did not believe this. Damn it! Their shouting must have awoken the baby, who started wailing as noisily as she was able. He took her tenderly in his arms and began to sing his favourite song:

'Somewhere over the rainbow...'

It always worked like a charm. Věrka immediately fell quiet, looking happy and contented. Tomáš realized just how much he loved her, and his soul whispered, *She understands.*

— • —

Early next morning he made love with Eliška. For the first time it struck him that this might be the last time, as everything could get out of hand. Because of this he fully felt the present moment. He realized that nothing but the present exists, at which point something broke down within him. It would never be the same again.

Their lovemaking had eased the tense atmosphere, but her disapproval of his involvement could still be felt in the air. During the morning the anticipated message arrived. The Prime Minister would meet them for a couple of minutes that evening. He began to prepare his things, when his wife tried it on him one more time.

'So you want to sacrifice everything?'

'Sometimes you have to, because of what you believe in,' he sighed heavily.

'It's not your fight. Darling, please don't go,' and she kissed him on the cheek. It almost broke him. He did not know whether to stay or go. For a while he wondered what would happen if he stayed home. He felt the security, but something told him it was all false. Again his soul spoke: *She is afraid for you. Of course, love is more important than fear. But let's go.* With tears in his eyes he kissed her and they embraced, whispering, 'I love you.'

'I love you too.'

— • —

He met up with Dimitri, Jirka and Kristýna outside No. 53, and they immediately set off. In the car they went over the ways they would talk with the Prime Minister. Jirka was rather cautious.

'We shouldn't speak too much about how we met and say that we believe in energy, meditation and all that. The Prime Minister is not the kind of person to understand that sort of thing, and it would undermine his confidence in us quite unnecessarily. We should focus on the fact that we have evidence, admittedly indirect, relating to serious criminal acts. Particularly the fact that Musílek is behind the disappearance of several people who stood in his way.'

Dimitri agreed. 'We should also explain to him that the only way to stop Musílek is to announce early elections. I would emphasize the fact that he probably has a hidden majority in parliament.'

Kristýna warned them of the possible dangers: 'When you are talking with the Prime Minister, focus on yourself and make sure you have enough energy. We will not have much time. If you feel any lack of faith in yourself or others including the Prime Minister then put three fingers together and remember the most wonderful experience that you have ever had.'

Tomáš immediately recalled when he first saw Eliška and Věrka in the hospital. His heart immediately began to beat faster and he felt a pleasant warmth flooding through him. As soon as they got to Prague they found themselves in a traffic jam. Tomáš admired Jirka's excellent knowledge of the local streets, as he wove his way through them to avoid being late. About an hour later they were in front of the Government Office. As they got out of the car, Tomáš began to feel nervous, so he put his three fingers together. It worked marvellously.

They let Jirka do the talking at reception, and after a brief security check they were shown upstairs to the Prime Minister's office, accompanied all the while by a security woman. The entire building looked several hundred years old, but it had been tastefully modernized. Tomáš had never taken advantage of his opportunity to come on a school visit. When they knocked on the Prime Minister's door, his assistant invited them in smilingly and asked them to bear with her for a moment.

They sat down on a large leather sofa and waited around five minutes until two people came out of the office. One of them looked like the Finance Minister. Tomáš realized that he was about to speak to a person to whom few people in the Czech Republic had immediate access. This flustered him, so again he put his three fingers together, and again it worked.

'You may go in now,' the assistant said, pointing to the door.

The Prime Minister was sitting in a leather armchair and drinking water. His study was spacious and clean. Lying on a glass table was a green file, bursting at the seams. He stood up from his armchair and offered his hand, first to Kristýna: 'Welcome.'

Jirka bowed his head. 'Good afternoon, Prime Minister.'

'Less of the formalities, Jirka,' the Prime Minister smiled.

After a couple more expressions of courtesy, Jirka briefly outlined why they were there. Others occasionally filled in for him, but the presentation was overall very persuasive. The Prime Minister thought it over and furrowed his balding brow. 'This is a very serious accusation and very disturbing indeed. Do you have any evidence?'

Jirka cautiously answered, 'We have contacted his former colleague, who's been living in hiding for a long time. He is willing to testify in front of a judge.'

But the Prime Minister was rather wary. 'I still don't want to believe this. I hope you won't take offence if I have this information vetted by the people I trust. Still, I've known you for years, and the way some of our party members have gone over to Musílek's new party does strike me as odd. I rather doubt the Labour and Justice Party's programme appeals to them that much. I have been out of the country recently, so I've not been entirely able to follow the recent goings-on. If what you say is true, then it has to be dealt with immediately.'

Kristýna sounded a note of warning: 'Do please be careful. We cannot even guess how many people Musílek has managed to manipulate.'

For a moment his reserve evaporated. 'Thank you, Kristýna. I have a few friends that I can always rely upon. If it is as you say it is, and Musílek manages to gain a majority in parliament then all he has to do is to express no confidence in my government and persuade the President to appoint him to form a new government.' He leant back into his armchair. 'It would be something of a non-standard situation, because the Labour and Justice Party has not previously been in parliament. I have never seen this happening anywhere before.'

'Of course, that doesn't mean it couldn't happen now,' Tomáš pointed out. 'Does the law allow for it?'

'Unfortunately, the constitution does not take this kind of situation into account at all, so he could indeed get into power this way. You have doubtless come to the same conclusion yourselves, otherwise you would not be here. So what do you suggest?'

Jirka finally got to the point of their visit. 'We think it would be best if you stepped down and announced early elections before Musílek gets into power.'

The Prime Minister tried to hide his surprise: 'But that would not entirely resolve the situation. He could easily win those early elections, and it would amount to the same thing.'

'Yes, it would,' said Dimitri, 'but it would give us two or three months, by which time we could have initiated court proceedings, which would turn public opinion against Musílek. After all, winning elections is a bit more complicated than blackmailing politicians.'

It was very difficult to make out what the Prime Minister was really thinking.

'It's a reasonable plan, but I am still not sure if he will get enough deputies in his new party. He would have to have some dirt on all of them. Moreover, if I give up power, I won't be able to influence what happens next.'

'We understand that,' Jirka assured him. 'We came to visit you today to tell you just how serious the situation is. Do please check to see if it applies to a large number of deputies. When it comes to the crunch, I know you'd rather resign than allow a murderer and dictator to get into power. I've known you for quite some time, so I am aware you're a decent person.'

The Prime Minister smiled sincerely. 'Thanks, Jirka, you are quite right. You can rest assured I will do what needs to be done. I thank you all for coming today. If your accusations prove right then you have risked a lot by coming here today. I shall do everything I can to make sure the cases are taken up by people we can trust. I would now like to ask you to go into seclusion, not to tell anybody else and not to expose yourselves to any needless risks. Watch out for yourselves. I assure you I will do everything for the good of us all.'

'Thank you, Prime Minister,' said Kristýna, offering her hand. After the others had said their good-byes, the security guards accompanied them to the doors. They were happy with the way the meeting had gone, and the conversation on the way back did not dry up. They counted how many times each of them had put their three fingers together and cracked a few jokes. There was an optimistic mood in the car.

That is, until the moment Jirka nervously muttered, 'I think we're being followed.'

They all looked at one other. Tomáš turned round, but could not see the suspect car.

Jirka glanced in the rear mirror: 'That black BMW. It's been behind us all the way from Prague. It might be a police car.'

Tomáš was watching the black car carefully. 'Do you think the Prime Minister might have had us followed?'

But before anybody managed to answer, the car overtook them and a STOP sign in the rear window started flashing. Dimitri yelled, 'Don't stop, it's a trap!'

Tomáš breathed faster. He wanted to advise Jirka, but he had no idea what. The car in front of them began to brake. If they wanted to get away, this was their last chance to do so. Dimitri kept repeating it was a trap. Jirka was confused. He lost his usual self-confidence and Kristýna's eyes were closed. And Tomáš? He had the impression he was going to jump out of his skin. He tried putting his three fingers together, but it did not help at all.

What if they kill us all now? His mind stopped working altogether as another thought overwhelmed it: Get away! Get away! Get away! He yelled at Jirka, 'Quick, get us out of here!'

This gave Jirka the confidence he needed. 'I'll overtake him and take off!' His right hand was reaching for the gear lever when he felt Kristýna gently touching it.

'Stop.' She looked tranquil and resolved.

'But what if...?' Dimitri stammered.

'Not now,' said Kristýna. 'Please stop, Jirka.'

He took his foot off the pedal and slowly began to brake. Tomáš calmed down a little and told himself they were probably just ordinary police who wanted to do a spot check.

The black BMW came to a halt just a couple of metres in front of them. Two men in police uniforms got out of it. Jirka wound down the window as they approached. One police officer with short, dark hair, looking something over thirty, was quite reserved.

'I need to see your papers.'

When Jirka started rummaging in the compartment, the police officer added, 'All of you.'

He gave all their documents to his older colleague, who examined them for a while and entered the data on a small computer. They spoke together for a few moments and then the older police officer tersely announced, 'All of you, come with us.'

'Why? What's going on?' Dimitri asked in alarm.

Before Tomáš managed to say anything, someone opened the door on his side of the car. He could not understand where this man in dark clothing had come from. Instinctively he looked behind and saw another two cars. He heard a noise from in front and saw a young police officer struggling with Dimitri.

Muscular arms grabbed Tomáš by the shirt and attempted to drag him out. He started defending himself and received a thump for his trouble. Using his leg he at least tried to stay in the car. He was holding on for all he was worth when he heard a woman's cry as they loaded Kristýna into the waiting car. This threw him off balance for a moment, and he literally flew out of the door and landed on his face on the wet asphalt. He howled in pain.

Two men picked him up and headed for their car. He started shouting for help and received another couple of punches in his stomach and his teeth. One of them gave him an emphatic warning. 'Better keep your mouth shut, sunshine. Or I'll kick your head in!'

He was handcuffed and a bag was put over his head, and then they literally threw him into the back seat, bruising his hand, so that again he cried out in pain.

'Get up, you sissy!'

Somebody sat down next to him and helped him up. The car slowly drove off. 'Shut your gob, don't cause any bother and you won't get hurt.' He felt humiliated, wronged and cheated. He was filled with anger. How could anyone dare?

He realized that neither Dimitri, Jirka nor Kristýna were in the car. So now he was all on his own.

'Where are you taking them?' he asked out loud, or did he just think it? He could think of nothing but awful things and was on the point of bursting out crying like a little child. He would have curled up into a little ball if he could. Before he was aware of what he was doing he spoke out loud. 'You can't just abduct us like this! You'll never get away with it!'

The man sitting beside him laughed out loud. 'Ah, sir is an idealist. Not to worry – we know how to deal with them too...'

So he thought better of it and fell silent. He did not know how long the journey took, but it seemed an eternity. When they took the bag off his head, the man did not wait for him to get accustomed to the light again, and threw him out. He fell twice before he could see beneath his feet. He was in a garage somewhere and being dragged up some stairs.

His escort knocked on a door and two armed men opened up. He must have looked ready to faint because they started taunting him:

'Hope you don't peg out here, deary, because dragging you upstairs is the last thing we want.'

He ended up handcuffed to a chair in a small dark room, immersed for a long time in the blackest of thoughts. He thought of Eliška and the baby: Dear God, please let me see them again.

— • —

He must have fainted from exhaustion, and he was only brought round by a very well-aimed slap. Smack! It stung horribly. The one that hit him stepped back and stood at the door. Opposite sat someone who was taunting him. 'Did you really think you could meet up with the Prime Minister without me finding out? Who do you think I am?'

He realized with horror who was sitting opposite. He wore a suit and a perfectly adjusted red necktie. Tomáš shook all over:

'H-How did you know?'

Musílek's smoothly shaven face was adorned by a smile. 'Let us say that one of my trusted friends tipped me off that the Prime Minister was being approached by people who would be of interest to me. So I did not hesitate and sent for you immediately. My diary is rather full,' and he put on an unctious expression. 'I hope you weren't planning anything for this evening. I want to have a little chat with you.' Raising his hand he added, 'Adam, please take the handcuffs off our guest.'

The doorman walked up at a slow, confident pace and undid the cuffs. Meanwhile Tomáš was wondering. Does Musílek know about Chrobák? He must not find out about him at any cost.

Stroking the abrasions on his wrist, he asked, 'Wh-where are the others? What have you done with them?'

'Hmm, they are safe, just as you are. Don't worry. What kind of host would I be? I just want information.'

Tomáš wondered if he said the same to all those he then killed. He decided it would be best to act like an idiot. 'I-I don't know what you're talking about.'

Musílek stood up and leant against the old wooden table.

'You probably know that I was a police officer for fifteen years. Whenever an interrrogation starts, people think that they can play dumb, and that I'm going to be taken in. Believe me, Mr Jedlička, I am not going to fall for that. You know very well why you are here,' and he leant forward towards him.

'But why am I here?!' Tomáš yelled out. The man by the door stepped towards him, this time at a brisk pace, and only stopped at his boss's gesture.

'Don't shout. Adam doesn't like it when people shout. You are here because you have had a lot of nonsense given to you; nonsense about me and what I am doing.'

'Well considering the way I got here I wouldn't say it's nonsense,' Tomáš let loose.

The corners of Musílek's mouth tightened in satisfaction. 'Ah, so you see, you do know something, Mr Jedlička.'

Now Tomáš was cursing himself. Why do I even try? Fool that I am. I don't have a chance against him. If he doesn't get it out of me by fair means then he can easily beat me up to find out. God, why oh why didn't I watch out more?

Musílek again insisted, 'Mr Jedlička, I know that you went to visit Karla Novotná, who escaped from prison immediately afterwards. I also know that you spoke to the Prime Minister about me. What did you tell him?'

Tomáš decided to change his tactics. He would cooperate and tell him all the information that an ordinary person might have heard from the television or easily put together.

'We went to see the Prime Minister, because you want to get into power. We wanted to warn him about you.'

'But why should I be a danger to him or to you?' Musílek retorted.

'Because you're a blackmailer and a kidnapper now too!' Tomáš roared. Adam quickly stepped in and in spite of Tomáš's resistance dealt him a blow to the stomach that a professional boxer would not have been ashamed of. This time Musílek did not stop him. A few seconds later Tomáš threw up.

'I told you, Mr Jedlička. I am the only one who can shout around here. You are not being the ideal guest,' and he pointed to Tomáš's lunch on the floor.

'Well, you are not being the ideal host,' said Tomáš, wiping the vomit around his mouth with his shirt. Tomáš was going to say something about Miloš, but fortunately this time he held back:

'There's proof!'

'And have you seen that proof, Mr Jedlíčka? Or did you just believe someone who talked about it?'

Tomáš lowered his gaze as his 'host' again gained the upper hand.

'Ah, you see. That is what is known as naivety.'

'But you did kill a man and then put the blame on Karla. How can you deny that?'

Musílek sat down in a chair and started tapping his fingers on the table. 'Hmm, is that what she told you? Do you really think I would have got away with that? Haven't you been rather taken in by her little drama performance? She always had a way with men – you have to give her that. Have a look at the facts. Check out the police files!'

Saying this, he threw a thick file onto the table. Then he got up again. 'These are the facts. Another fact is that your friends have been trying to deceive you all along. You ought to be more careful about what you believe from what a criminal has to say.'

Tomáš briefly glanced at the police files. It was Marek's track record.

He had committed fraud and been in prison several times. Next to the file was a record of finger prints on the weapon that had shot that fleeing burglar. The prints belonged to Karla.

'Ah yes, but then if you're so innocent, why have you abducted us like this?'

'I have a lot of enemies. Many people do not like the fact that I plan to do away with corruption. Sometimes I am hard, but I would never actually hurt anybody. Is there anything else you would like to tell me?' He rubbed his hands and Tomáš drew a breath, but eventually lowered his gaze and fell silent.

Musílek eyed him triumphantly: 'You got mixed up in all this quite by chance, didn't you, Mr Jedlička? Now you run along home. This isn't your fight. This isn't any of your business. Leave it to me.'

At the door he remembered something else:

'And Mr Jedlička, next time please address me as "Prime Minister".'

A short while later, Tomáš was sitting in the car (how else but with a sweaty bag over his head?). He had calmed down a little. He now realized that he had been playing a game all along. His place was at home with his family. This was just a play he should not have been in. It turned out Musílek was not as bad as he had appeared all that time. After all, he had let them go home, unless he was now going to have them shot somewhere outside the city limits. When he realized this he was again scared to death.

The car stopped, somebody handed him his mobile phone and whispered, 'Better not tell anyone about today. Your wife and daughter are often home alone, aren't they?'

When they threw him out of the vehicle, it took him a while to find his bearings. He was several streets away from his home. He immediately called Jirka, Kristýna and Dimitri to see if they were all right, and breathed a sigh of relief when he heard their voices.

'I am glad you are all right, Tom. We can go over it tomorrow at No. 53,' said Jirka, ending the conversation.

He agreed to a meeting, but immediately started to regret it. He felt sorry he had got involved in all this. Eliška was right. With the last of his strength he limped back home. She and the baby were sleeping soundly. When he saw them he leant against a wall, slowly slipped down it to the ground and burst out crying. Then he headed straight to the shower. He had to wash everything off, particularly the vomit. The hot water streamed down his trembling body and only very slowly washed off the horror he had experienced that day. But it did not wash off everything. You carry something like that around with you for the rest of your life.

3/26 The interview

Tomáš half-opened his eyes. His entire body was feeling sore, but that was nothing compared with what he experienced when he sat down. His stomach clenched up tight, as if someone had punched it with all their might. It hurt like hell! Eventually he managed to stand. Eliška was feeding the baby in the kitchen. 'I was afraid for you yesterday. I was relieved when I woke up today to see you lying next to me. But you look awful. Has anything happened to you?'

He had a choice. He could have protected her by not saying anything, but he decided to come out with the truth. He gulped down some water and said, 'It didn't go very well.'

'How come? Did the Prime Minister not believe you?' and she put the baby on her shoulder.

'It went better than we expected with the Prime Minister, but then Musílek had us all picked up, and he tried to get us to reveal what we have on him.'

'What? Good God!' Eliška cried out. 'Are you all right? Did you report it to the police?' The baby started to cry.

He put the glass down and supported himself with his hands against the table. It had certainly not been a good idea to have a drink of water. He managed to say: 'Ugh, I haven't reported anything, and please don't tell anyone else. I only told you so that I didn't have to lie.'

'Why don't you report it to the police? There were several of you after all. That means several witnesses!' And she stroked Věrka's back.

'I might have talked as naively as that yesterday, but not after what's happened. We mustn't tell anybody about it. We have to protect ourselves and Věrka,' he said dejectedly. 'From now on I shall take far more care. I was an idiot. Forgive me.'

Eliška still had the baby in her arms when he embraced her. As he hugged them affectionately, his eyes misted over again. He finally understood what family meant to him.

He preferred to go to No. 53 on an empty stomach, and wondered if this was the last time he would be seeing the team. He felt distrust towards Marek and Karla after what Musílek had shown him. He was among the last to arrive, and without waiting he launched into Marek.

'How come you never said you'd been in prison?'

'Well, you never asked,' Marek calmly answered.

'You shitter, what else have you not told us yet? And why didn't Karla tell us that her fingerprints were on that gun?'

Karla was outraged by this accusation. 'Do you think I did it? You know you were taking a risk when you went to see the Prime Minister. I don't know what Musílek told you, but I don't understand why you believe him.'

'Because he let me read your records.'

'Well, of course he has evidence that I did it. Otherwise I wouldn't have been put in prison. I just don't understand how you could have let yourself be led astray so easily. That is just unforgivable,' and she gave him a withering look.

Kristýna intervened before he could respond: 'That's enough of that. That is exactly what Musílek wants. We must be a real threat for him to risk abducting us like that. Let's stick together. We are very close to accomplishing our task.'

Dimitri agreed. 'The abduction yesterday only proves it. Marek is an idiot for not telling us, but now that doesn't matter. As for Karla, Musílek tried that on me too.'

'And on me,' Kristýna added. 'But I looked into his eyes when he did, and I knew he was lying.'

Karla calmed down a little: 'Thank you for not doubting me.'

Tomáš clasped his hands to his head and sighed out loud. 'But how can I believe you? Do you have nothing but your word?'

Kristýna looked at him affectionately. 'What does your heart tell you?'

He became absorbed in his thoughts and remembered his childhood, when he accidently cut his sister's hand. Their mother went crazy. She was really angry with him. It seemed like just the other day when his dad came up and stroked her hand. 'We all make mistakes. That's what makes us people, my dear.'

He came back to the present. 'My heart tells me we all make mistakes. We should not allow our mistakes to divide us.'

Kristýna's eyes shone when she heard this. Dimitri nodded in appreciation: 'So let's get to work. There's a lot for us to do.'

Jirka began with the most important matters. 'Did you say or did anybody indicate that we are in contact with Miloš?'

Dimitri, Kristýna and Tomáš looked at him and said they had not.

He breathed a sigh of relief. 'That's good. Very good. That is what I feared most. I'm glad we managed to keep that quiet. It could be the decisive trump in this round.'

As always, Marek had some fresh information:

'According to my information the Labour and Justice Party will try to force a vote of no confidence on the government today. And today the media are to receive a report on the charges against Musílek regarding several abductions and murders.'

'So it looks like today is our D-Day. That irascible old git has pulled it off,' said Jirka.

'I think we can help. We can give the media an interview about what happened yesterday. We can say out loud that we were abducted. Then we can give the police the recording,' said Kristýna.

'First we can get it broadcast on TV, so the police don't lose it,' Marek quipped.

Dimitri stroked his beard: 'It would be very audacious and dangerous, but it might work. That is just what Musílek is not expecting, for someone to stand up in public against him undaunted.'

Tomáš cautiously pointed out, 'That is quite risky. All of us here have families. We have to carefully consider if the risk is worth it. I don't want anybody to harm my wife and children.'

Jirka added, 'That is true. It's a dangerous game. Either it works and Musílek goes to jail, or we're up against it for a very long time to come.'

'I am well aware of that,' said Dimitri, 'just as I am aware that I am not only endangering myself, but if I said no then I would be going against everything I have been advocating all my life. So I'm in.'

Kristýna also agreed, 'Whenever my mind says no and my heart says yes, I always listen to my heart.'

Tomáš recalled the dream in which he lost his soul. 'I'd rather live all my life in uncertainty than lose my soul.' And he felt it stirring within him. *Thank you. I love you.*

Jirka had also made his decision: 'If we don't succeed then I lose my business, my good name and my sense of security. Even worse, my family would be in a very difficult position. Sorry, but I think you'll understand. Naturally I'll help you any way I can, but I will not testify.'

Kristýna nodded. 'We understand, and we appreciate your help. Without you we would never have got this far.'

Dimitri put on his coat as he explained, 'I have friends in television. I think it will definitely be worthwhile to record an interview with them.'

It was a clear and beautiful autumn day. Eliška was outside with Věrka, so Tomáš was able to pack without interruption for his trip to Brno, where Dimitri's friend was meant to be waiting for him at the studio. He was soon assailed by doubts again. Just that morning he had not wanted to get involved in anything else, and now he was doing the precise opposite. What happened when he last showed such naivety? What if Musílek got to find out? What would he say to the camera? After all, he was not at all prepared for this.

His soul was to be heard: *Leave it to me.*

They were waiting in a conference room when an attractive young reporter appeared in the doorway. Her light brown curly hair perfectly matched her childlike face. She looked around eighteen, but her style of dress and manner indicated that she was at least twenty-five. She invited Dimitri into the studio first, while Tomáš was last in line for an interview. He was nervous, but after a while he got used to the camera. Iveta first asked him a few things about Musílek and the abduction. Tomáš was also interested in how she got to know Dimitri and what she was actually doing in television.

'Since I left school I've been involved in investigative journalism. I read a few of his books, which very much appealed to me, so we've been seeing each other regularly ever since. He's a very inspiring man.'

'Yes, he is,' Tomáš agreed.

Then Iveta moved on to some personal questions: 'Aren't you afraid? Obviously, you are risking your life by sitting here today and speaking to the camera.'

He answered as he felt fit. 'I am afraid, but that doesn't stop me from doing something that I believe is the right thing to do.'

'How did you get to know these people?'

He described what had happened since he had got to know Naďa. He knew that some people would not believe this, but he did not care.

He was happy to speak as he felt fit. His narrative ended with the abduction.

'What impression did Mr Musílek make on you during this interrogation?'

'First he tried to intimidate me and then after a while he started acting like my best friend. He said it wasn't my fight and that I should leave it all to him. That is precisely what is so dangerous about him. It is very easy to fall for his charisma and his spurious concern, but all he is really interested in is his own personal advantage. Anyone who has a different view to his has to get out of his way. One way or another. I'm not surprised at the people who let themselves be taken in by him. I believed him myself for a while, so I'm not guilt-free myself. I believed him that it's not my fight.'

'And is it your fight?'

'It is everybody's fight. If we fight for a better world, we show each other that we are human. If we fight for what we believe is right then are actually alive.'

'Why are you doing this? Why are you taking such a risk? Aren't you afraid for the safety of your family and yourselves?'

'It is precisely because I have somebody important in my life that I am sitting here with you. It's only a pity that my wife and daughter aren't here with me. I would very much like you to get to know them. Even an idiot like me has had the good fortune to have such a marvellous family. I want my daughter to grow up in a free and just world. I want Věrka to grow up in a world where instead of telling her what to think and how to feel, others are interested in what she feels. A world without intimidation and one-sided solutions. A world where happiness is the meaning of life. If you are only interested in results, but not in how they are achieved then that is bad. We have to take some risks and make sure that people like Mr Musílek do not get into power in this country.'

'Isn't that all a little naive?' asked Iveta.

'It is naive to think that we can carry on the same lifestyle as we have previously. It is naive to think that humanity can survive the problems that we face without love, understanding and caring for one another. It is also naive to think that we can use violence on others, without ourselves being harmed.'

'What kind of problems do you have in mind?'

'I have dreams that have been recurring for some time now. In all of these dreams people are struggling for their bare existence. They burrow down in underground shelters, and such things as hope, faith, trust and love have disappeared. I don't want to live in a world where people have forgotten what they are.'

'And do you think that all this will really happen?'

'If people listen to their hearts, forgive themselves after each lapse, dust themselves down and carry on where their souls are taking them, then this will certainly not happen. If we fight then we have nothing to fear. If we use our hearts as weapons then we become something greater. We will make this world much more than it is now. Much more than we can imagine in our most wonderful imaginings. We can create a heaven on earth. I am here to remind people of this, just as a friend of mine used to remind me.'

'Thank you, Tomáš.'

After the interview they chatted for a while, and amongst other things he showed her a photo of Eliška and Věrka. Then Iveta confided, 'This interview went in a completely different direction to what I originally intended. But that doesn't matter one bit. You made a great impression on me. Watch out for yourself, Tom!'

He embraced her and said: 'I'm glad there are people like you in the world. Look after yourself.'

— • —

When he got home the first thing he did was to give Eliška a big hug. She was quite put out by this, and both of them had tears in their eyes and did not say anything, because no words were needed. Then he went to have a look at the baby, who was sleeping, so he gave her an affectionate kiss on the forehead and lay down on the bed for a while. It's been a long day, he thought, and his eyelids slowly drooped. He felt fine, despite the fact that (or perhaps because) he had done something as bold as that. It was Eliška who woke him up.

'Now it's started!'

Musílek stood at a podium with the Labour and Justice Party logo showing a lion with a hammer in its hand. Tomáš had to think for a moment before he remembered where he had seen that symbol. Then he recalled with horror that he had glimpsed it on a patch worn by one of his abductors. Under the logo was the inscription: Work and justice for everybody. He had not caught the beginning of the speech, so it took him a while to start putting everything together:

'... in this position I have always tried to honestly and boldly confront bribery, rule breaking and human stupidity. Nevertheless I also have to admit that I failed in this task! Hence I left the police force and for a long time I sought to find evidence that our society, and our state, is not that badly off. Unfortunately, I did not find any evidence. The politicians at the top are corrupt. Criminals laugh at our judicial system and the ordinary person who works hard to feed his family is worse off than any loafer.'

Musílek's speech was very seductive. Tomáš found it just as persuasive as he did that time in the cellar. He would have swallowed his every word if he did not know his hidden face.

'For me it is important where this society, this country, is heading. As a decent and hard-working citizen I cannot just stand by and watch!' and he leant on his podium the same way as when he was interrogating Tomáš. 'Hence I have decided to join the party which I believe can change it. I have decided to join the Labour and Justice

Party.' The hall was filled with the hum of people whispering to each other.

'We have agreed that tomorrow we shall demand a vote of no confidence in the current government. It is corrupt, remote from the problems of ordinary people and incapable of dealing with the fundamental issues that beset this country. You will find our political programme on our website. I appeal to all parliamentary deputies who are not indifferent to goings-on in this country to arise!' and he raised his arm to urge them on. 'To demonstrate their disapproval. Because I am a man of honour, and I am aware that everybody deserves a second chance, I have a generous offer for our deputies,' and he cast his gaze around the hall, as if they were all sitting there. 'If you are prepared to work hard on yourself, you are willing to sacrifice your good name for the good of society and you feel that you are not fully appreciated in your current party, then come over to us. Become a member of the Labour and Justice Party,' he thundered. 'You can expect a lot of work and much resistance from the people who are sucking this society dry, so think it over carefully. Whoever decides to join us can expect their first test within our ranks. As this government faces a vote of no confidence I ask you for your support.' And the people in the hall began to talk out loud to one other. 'If I get into power, I promise I will not leave one stone unturned,' he gestured emphatically. 'I will make it hot for the corrupt, reduce unemployment and make sure all the criminals and rapists are behind bars. I shall make this country as prosperous and as secure as you the citizens deserve it to be. Thank you.'

As he left the podium the journalists invited him to answer their questions, but he did not respond and walked off backstage. A beautiful, young woman now stood beside the podium. 'Please excuse Mr Musílek. He has a lot of important business to deal with today, as you can imagine. I will answer your questions and you will find other information on our web pages.'

The television programme returned to the studio, where the presenters gave their immediate reactions. 'In view of the current situation we have decided to follow developments non-stop. Stay tuned to our live broadcasting. We now go over to politologist Martin Zelený, who will no doubt give us his independent...'

Tomáš turned off the television and Eliška had difficulty finding the right words. 'I still cannot believe it, but if people get the information about the accusations against Musílek, then surely the deputies won't join him?'

'They have a difficult choice ahead of them. He has dirt on all of them and he's blackmailing them.'

'Good God! That can't be right. Is it that easy to get into power?'

'If people stop listening to their hearts then yes, it is. Fortunately, we can still avert this. The deputies are hiding away in the crowd. They won't admit that their own decision can change anything. They have the feeling that everybody else is going to vote for Musílek anyway. Fortunately not all of them are resigned to this happening. The Prime Minister can change everything with a single decision... if he decides to resign and go for early elections.'

'And will he do that?'

'I think he will. He looked determined.'

During the afternoon, there were reports on television that the police had received information about a possible link between Musílek and the disappearance of several people, but the charges against him were still under review. When Tomáš thought about this he came to the conclusion that the people who were to make the charges were holding back to see how the situation developed.

The Prime Minister's press spokesman announced that the vote of no confidence would take place the following day and that the Prime Minister would arrange a press conference beforehand. The journalists and invited experts agreed that it was not a standard procedure to call a press conference beforehand like that. There was also considerable debate over whether or not the accusations against Musílek were based on truth. Opinions varied on this.

However, most of the invited guests and experts agreed that things were developing in a very unusual manner. It is not normal for a small party with practically no influence to get into power overnight. All without proper electoral procedures. This provoked conflicting reactions among the guests. Some of them expressed the opinion that Musílek was a publicly recognized figure, and well-liked among the people, who would probably vote for him in elections, so that the specific way he got into power was of no importance. If Musílek did away with corruption and put the economy in order then people would hardly be worried about how he got into power.

In the evening Jirka called to invite him over for a meeting a couple of hours later. The Prime Minister had called a press conference for four the next day, and both agreed that this was the key moment. That night he could not get to sleep for a long time. He wondered for some time why their testimony on the recent abduction had not been broadcast on television. Where was Miloš now? Would it all work out? What if it did not? That was not a pleasant thought. Still, eventually he fell asleep.

3/27 The key moment

At the meeting Dimitri gave them some bad news. 'The video of our interviews will not be appearing on TV. Iveta apologizes to us all, but the TV administration do not want the recording to be broadcast. They say they don't want to influence public opinion.'

'So Musílek has his people in television,' said Tomáš.

'It looks that way,' said Marek.

'The worst of it is that she tried to find the recordings and copy them for possible use in future,' said Dimitri. 'She says there's something fishy going on too. The recordings have disappeared, along with the evidence. As if they had never been made.'

'Good God,' said Karla, 'what are we going to do?'

'There's nothing left to do but wait and hope that people choose correctly and that the Prime Minister supports their choice,' said Dimitri.

'How do you mean?'

'You know, I was thinking about what we were talking about last time. Today people are going to decide whether or not they want Musílek in power. As he is sure of the deputies' votes, the only person who can stop him at this moment is the Prime Minister. This is a fine example of an individual having far more power than the crowd. At this moment he is holding the proverbial balance. He will incline whichever way the people subconsciously want to go. The Prime Minister will subconsciously direct his steps in accordance with their decision. Hence the key moment is his press conference. I am not worried about the Prime Minister's resolve, but I'm not sure what the people are going to choose.'

'If the people go for Musílek then it is a practically irreversible choice,' said Tomáš.

'We have to help them make it,' Kristýna said in the doorway as she arrived. She took off her coat and continued: 'I have been thinking over the decision-making process that you were telling us about last time. It is quite complex. There's an enormous number of variables, such as the influences of the seasons, lunar cycles, the current psychological state of the person involved, the overall mood within society, expectations and the like. It really is complicated. One element is the free will within us all, which is then reflected in the collective choice. The second thing is that our decision may be influenced by other people and all these variables.'

Marek agreed. 'Your description is complicated enough.'

'So what have you concluded?' asked Tomáš.

'That it is much simpler than it appears. We need not know all the variables, the weight each has and the relations between them. This system is so complex that we will never manage to understand it in its entirety.'

'So what does all that mean then?' Karla asked. 'Don't keep us in suspense.'

'Simply that in a system where some fundamental choice is being made, all you have to add is a sufficient quantum of love.'

Tomáš was interested. 'And how does that work exactly?'

'If we succeed in adding a sufficient amount of energy for a critical number of people to choose correctly, their choice causes a chain reaction. People who are in two minds or who are going to vote without being fully aware are then inspired by them. It is then enough for the Prime Minister to accede to their choice and to call for early elections in his speech.'

Dimitri did not hide his enthusiasm. 'That is a completely different view of choices to the one I've developed over the years, but I have to admit there is something in it. How do we accomplish all that though?'

Kristýna smiled at him. 'We wait for the others and form a meditation group to connect with the system. We then try to find the most suitable candidates, and we send them our energy.'

'The others will be here in a while,' said Karla. 'Meantime we can prepare.'

Marek started to probe. 'And why can't we just send energy out to the Prime Minister?'

'It doesn't work like that,' said Kristýna. 'We might achieve a short-term victory, but from the long-term perspective you need to keep supplying energy to the system as a whole.'

Tomáš started thinking out loud. 'How come I didn't think of supplying energy to the system like this earlier?! If you don't have enough energy then your mind clouds over. You can't make out the consequences of your own choice very clearly. The more love and energy you have, the more clearly your mind knows what your choice will result in. The entire process of decision-making, which otherwise remains unconscious, now becomes conscious.'

'You become awoken,' said Dimitri.

Marek described the same thing in other words. 'The more energy you have, the more accurately your mind can process information and so the more accurate is the calculation of the future that it performs, thus making it all a conscious process. You realize how your actions impact other people, which makes it a clear-minded choice for you.'

'Right, people normally refer to this as intuition,' added Kristýna, 'without actually knowing how it operates.'

'The more energy you have within yourself,' said Tomáš, 'the more people you manage to inspire – and affect their choices. You obtain energy either by learning to generate it within yourself and thus being a model, or you learn to steal it from others, by intimidating and humiliating them and that kind of thing. If you really have a lot of energy then you can influence millions of people, like the Dalai Lama or Mother Teresa...'

'Or Hitler,' Marek interrupted.

'Or Hitler. But he stole his energy. Collective choices like the one that awaits us soon always have far greater consequences and become set in stone more rapidly. For something complex to be set in stone, you have to supply it with energy over the long term and not go choosing this or that every once in a while.'

'Or you have to truly make it a collective decision,' said Dimitri.

Kristýna could not contain her enthusiasm. 'It's amazing how it works!' She started to place the chairs and armchairs in a circle and the others immediately assisted.

A voice came from the doorway: 'Better prepare seven places.' It was Naďa, who had arrived together with Jirka. 'I could not miss out on this. If you allow me to help you it will be an honour. Just to look at you, I see you have come a long way since we last saw each other. You make me very glad.'

Before they began, Kristýna warned them, 'No way are you to advise anybody on how to decide. Please just supply them with energy. We are not here to make decisions for other people. Even though we will feel somewhere inside what is best for a particular person, we must not force him to make that choice. The least pressure may result in the precise opposite of what we want. Now let's get down to it! Please take each other by the hand.'

After a brief hubbub as they took their seats, a silence descended upon the room. The fragrances of incense sticks and freshly baked biscuits mixed in the air, as Kristýna began:

'Close your eyes and relax. Breathe in deeply and breathe out slowly. You have come a long way to get here. It was challenging and strewn with obstacles, but without them you would not have become what you are today – a being full of love and understanding. A being that has seen through the mist of everyday light and seen the light within us all – a god.

All your life you have been preparing for this moment. Everything has been focused on this instant. Imagine that you are sitting at an old wooden table. You are musing beneath an enormous, sturdy oak tree, which has started to awake after a long winter. The sun is warming your face pleasantly. In front of you on the table is a blank piece of paper, and you have a pencil in your hand. You may begin to write or draw on it, to doodle or to do a portrait. Or you can leave it blank. You can do whatever you want. You could start to write any story...'

Tomáš was sitting opposite a young mother who was peeling potatoes at a kitchen table. She was tired – her younger son had been sick during the night and had been crying throughout. She had been with him all that time, comforting him. Now she was overwrought. She still had to deal with so many things today. On the radio she was listening to the news about the political situation. She thought: All the politicians are corrupt and just getting money out of us. I have less money on maternity benefit with the second child than with just the one. Is that fair? If Musílek got into power, he would definitely change that.

Tomáš understood her. He would have felt the same way in her situation. He did not hold her decision against her at all. A magnificent light was hidden within her. All night she had taken care of the child. She had not slept and now it was daytime she was looking after the other one. All of this without a single negative thought for her children. He admired her. Then something happened that he did not expect. Their hearts merged. He felt heavenly joy that he could now display his unique soul. He was overwhelmed by the beautiful, multicoloured soul of the mother. When they again separated he was pervaded by a sense of sadness over the loss of such a fulfilling union, but he soon came round. The mother's soul now appeared purer, more radiant. She quickened a little and thought: Still, not all politicians are the same. I can't tar them all with the same brush. Anyway, who knows what this Musílek is like? His former colleague is accusing him of blackmailing his opponents. What if that's true? What if he gets into power and gets rid of the people that don't agree with him that way? And what if one of them were close to me?

Tomáš observed the mass of people. There were so many that he could not watch them all at once. They stood in a kind of triangle. At one corner there was the mother he had just visited. Before her were her two children and husband. Before each of their children there were several of their friends' and neighbours' children. Before her husband stood his family and workmates. The further the mother looked, the fewer people she recognized, until at the very end there were thousands of people.

He blinked and found himself somewhere else completely. He was in the office of a young police officer working as a criminologist. Many of his experienced colleagues had left – they did not like the reduction in salary and their limited security, so they had simply left.

Now he was investigating the rape of a girl and he was extremely angry. This crime had clearly been committed by the same perpetrator as last time. They had been after him for several months, but he kept well clear of them! The police officer thought: If the government had not approved the budget reduction that time, my colleagues would have stayed and helped me with this case. Now here is another woman who is going to bear the consequences for the rest of her life. It's my fault too! And he banged the table, where there was a newspaper that described the current political situation.

He thought: If Musílek were in power, as the former Police Commissioner he would bring back the dignity and respect that all the police deserve. Then my colleagues would probably come back. The murderers and rapists would be put in prison much more quickly. Tomáš felt the pain the police officer was experiencing. He had failed! And because of his failure another girl had been raped. It was totally logical to ask for Musílek to get into power. The police officer was a clever, hard-working and upstanding man.

Tomáš admired him, and the next second he became him! He saw all the good that he had achieved during his career. He saw how many people he had helped. All his life he had shone brightly and made the world a better place. He had always behaved with respect and humility. Suddenly the connection was broken. Again Tomáš was sad and wanted it to last longer. The police officer thought: Leave it out! I'm doing everything in my power, I have an excellent team, and we will get this rapist eventually. He won't rape any more women. I've never actually liked Musílek. Back when he was Police Commissioner he only wanted results from us. He was never interested in how we achieved them. I always had the feeling that his concern for others was just a game. Then he came up with several ideas on how to catch the criminal, and he ran off immediately to go over them with his colleagues.

Tomáš was again watching hundreds of people. His police officer stood at the very start, followed by his friends, family and the people closest to him. Beyond that he did not recognize so many of them. As he looked at the triangular shape he noticed it was different to the previous one. At one end there was a rectangle-like structure. This was several times larger than the triangle and extended into the distance without any visible end. He could at least examine the connection between the triangle and the rectangle, where he saw a well-known face. He realized after a moment that this was a man he knew from the television.

Now Tomáš found himself back at No. 53, but still in a state of deep meditation. He saw seven beings sitting in a circle with light radiating from each of them. As soon as each light combined with those next to it, it became far more intensive, forming a magnificent multicoloured structure that resembled nothing he had ever seen before. Rays of light shot out all over the country to points where smaller structures again began to shoot out rays. It was all so marvellous! After some time the light flooded the entire country. It worked like a chemical reaction in which they were the catalysts.

He awoke with a single very powerful thought: Success! They had succeeded! Hooray! He rubbed his eyes and looked around him. They were all awake with a smile on their faces but wordless. They were just sitting and looking at each other. Then Karla said impatiently, 'So? Shall we turn on the TV and watch the Prime Minister's press conference?'

By way of answer the others turned their chairs and armchairs towards the television. The speech was due in less than fifteen minutes, so they chatted in the meantime, as discussions and interviews with experts were broadcast on what the Prime Minister intended to announce at the press conference. Considering the way the quite stable arrangements at the Chamber of Deputies had begun to collapse, the experts expected the Prime Minister to go for early elections, as most of them believed that the Labour and Justice Party did not have a sufficient mandate from the voters.

The press conference called by the Prime Minister began on time. He welcomed all those present and began his speech.

The Choice

'Our country has arrived at a very important juncture. Former Police Commissioner Musílek has decided to become a member of the Labour and Justice Party while urging deputies to support a vote of no confidence in the government that I am leading. The closer we come to the Chamber of Deputies session, the more deputies publicly declare support for the Labour and Justice Party. If we do not win the vote of no confidence, the creation of a new government might be entrusted to a party that received a mere 6% of our citizens'votes at the last elections.' He fell silent for a while and adjusted his spectacles. 'The way these deputies have all gone over to this small party has been very strange to say the least, so I have had to decide whether to permit these changes or to intervene. In view of the dubious mandate given to this new party the only way for me to intervene is to go for early elections,' and he sighed deeply. 'Believe me, I have never had a more difficult decision to make in my life. After careful consideration of all possible aspects I have decided not to intervene in the situation. I believe that over the next few hours, the deputies will decide as they think best.'

The people in the hall started to submit their questions to the Prime Minister. Everybody at No. 53 stared in surprise at the television set. Tomáš felt as if his best friend had shot him in the back of the neck.

'What? What's all this about? I know for absolute sure that people wanted the opposite.'

Kristýna confirmed. 'I don't understand either. I felt that people didn't want Musílek in power as well.'

Dimitri spoke up. 'If people didn't want him in power, and yet the Prime Minister did not listen to them, then it means...'

Tomáš finished off for him, '...that the Prime Minister has failed and given way to the pressure.'

Jirka objected, 'I've known him for years. He would never do that!'

Marek guiltily lowered his gaze. 'I didn't want to worry you unnecessarily, but...'

'What?' Karla looked at him scathingly.

Marek stammered, 'Just this morning, I gained access to Musílek's data, which he's been guarding with his life, so for a long time I have not been able to get into it. He had it really well protected. As soon as I succeeded, I realized why he was so careful. It included data on the most important people in the country. All this time we have been presuming that he'd not got to the top people, but he'd actually just hidden this information very deep.'

This really enraged Dimitri, who turned bright red. 'What did you find, Marek?'

'Everything about the Prime Minister, the President and their families. Special attention was particularly paid to observing his two daughters. There were lots of photos and several long videos, from the school and the ballet that one of them went to, as well as the parties she was at. I also found out how Musílek operated. He gave various people individual tasks, but none of them could guess what it was all in aid of. He took advantage of this. By the time they had put the overall picture together it was far too late.'

Jirka sat back in his chair resignedly. 'The bastard threatened to harm his children!'

Tomáš was also rather angry. 'Marek, it's happened several times now that you have kept something hidden from us and caused us problems. What did you have in mind when you didn't tell us?'

'Well it was too late to change anything anyway,' he defended himself.

Dimitri turned ever redder. 'If we'd only known then we could have tried to stop it. We might not have succeeded, but we could definitely have tried. Always tell us everything you find out, Marek. Damn it! Whatever you may think about it. That was our agreement. Can you imagine what you've done?!'

In contrast, Karla was as white as a sheet. 'Fools that we are, how could we have thought that Musílek would take such a risk. He knew very well that he had to have the Prime Minister on his side, so that's how he arranged things.'

'What are we going to do now?' asked Marek in alarm.

Karla had given up. 'There's nothing left to do but pray for a miracle this evening.'

But Tomáš had not. 'Do you want to just let it be like that? I'm not giving up that easily! We have to talk to the deputies...'

Dimitri interrupted him. 'If the Prime Minister was afraid to go against the flow, do you think the deputies hiding away in the crowd are going to listen to you? How do you think that he has threatened them? In exactly the same way. I think that the best we can do now is to go home and mull it over. Perhaps in the meantime the case based on Miloš's testimony will be brought against Musílek.'

Tomáš smiled ironically. 'Come on, Dimitri! You know very well that is nonsense. If he has managed to own the Prime Minister then he will certainly have that case sewn up.'

Only now did it hit Marek. 'Fuck, I have really screwed this up!'

Karla looked daggers at him. 'Your remorse is no good to us!'

Kristýna tried to calm them down: 'Hey, leave that out. There's no point. Let's go home and try to meet up again next week, after we have mulled it over a little. We may come up with something.'

When Tomáš got back home he had to keep coming back to it. He thought about the vote of no confidence in the government. All that is needed for evil to succeed is for each of us to make a small concession. And how could the Prime Minister have betrayed them like that? The world is so unpredictable. It often just takes one man to change everything, he sighed.

3/28 Unquiet world

The following day Tomáš did not feel very well – indeed he felt increasingly worse. Until now he had had a clear goal: to stop Musílek. But now his life lacked all meaning, and he slowly fell into a deeper and deeper depression. The worst part of it was that he was beginning to lose all hope that things would ever start improving. The Chamber of Deputies gave a vote of no confidence in the government and the President entrusted Musílek with forming a new government. Miloš had disappeared entirely. Who knew whether it was of his own free will or not? Fortunately, he had one piece of good news. Robert's parents had withdrawn their complaint against him, so he could at least go back to school. The headmistress had no idea why, and nobody else knew either. It was not much for him to hold on to.

Meanwhile the worldwide situation was getting much worse. Civil war had broken out in Nigeria, where the Christians and the Muslims were murdering each other by the thousands. All humanitarian organizations had to leave the country, because their safety could no longer be guaranteed. Experts believed other African countries would soon follow suit.

Mass anti-government protests were taking place in Russia and China. Even though the regimes there were fiercely suppressing the demonstrations, the number of protesters continued to increase. They wanted a new system of government, but everyone had their own ideas about what kind. Tensions were starting to grow throughout Europe, as most people's economic situations deteriorated and their prospects for the future were not at all cheerful. Europeans were being panicked into taking out their savings, so the banking system was on the brink of collapse. People were beset by increasing fear and uncertainty over what the future would bring. The worst situation seemed to be in the south-east. Many politicians and religious leaders had seized the opportunity to point the finger at those responsible. In some places it was the Jews and elsewhere the Roma or Muslims, and some countries blamed their neighbours. In Spain an ultraclerical movement was gaining in strength – as the One Law Party blamed its economic and social problems on the profligate lifestyles to be seen in modern-day society.

Nor was the situation any easier in Western Europe. Belgium fell apart into two states. Holland and France were convulsed by civil disturbances. Islamic radicals planned to turn both states into lands faithful to the Koran and agitated against the governments there. Their greatest success was among young unemployed Muslims, and of course this heightened the antagonism of Europeans towards Muslims not only in France and Holland but elsewhere too. In Romania and Bulgaria the state defended the Roma with all its strength. The majority wanted to forcibly expel them from the country and the police found it difficult to resist this onslaught. The numbers rose of those murdered, and the police did not manage to investigate them, because of the undertow within its own ranks.

Australia, Japan and South Korea did not have this kind of problem, but it did not do them much good, because their citizens lived in constant fear of nuclear attack from North Korea. It was officially stated that they had built their own bombs, but it was rumoured that China had provided them. Relations between Japan and China were at freezing point.

The gulf expanded between the young people who were demanding justice and corruption-free politics and the older people who did not like where society was heading, the upshot of which was that people no longer had any understanding for each other, barricaded within their movements and unable to see the viewpoints of their counterparts. The same tensions were carried over into families. One member did not understand the other and within a short space of time many families fell apart completely. Suddenly everyone was further apart. People were afraid to make any binding decision, such as moving house, conceiving children or changing job.

The situation was not that serious all over the world, but if war flared up in one of these trouble spots then it would have an effect on the entire planet. The Arabs had their allies and the European old guard had theirs. The Communists had their allies and the nationalists had theirs. Eastern Europe had Russia and Western Europe had the USA. Likewise the Chinese government had its allies and the protesters had theirs, so countries all over the world began to group together, and this caused unprecedented problems at the United Nations. The UN Council lost all power and the entire community of nations lost all meaning. Nobody could predict how the overall situation would develop.

— • —

Tomáš woke up and considered all this before he opened his eyes. It occurred to him to connect to the system just as he had done with the team, but this time not just to focus on the Czech Republic. It was Saturday and Eliška had taken the baby to her parents, so it was quiet enough at home. Outside it was still dark. The days were getting shorter as winter approached. He lit several candles and a fragrant lamp. Gradually he succeeded in excluding all thoughts and a short time later he felt that he was hovering in the air somewhere.

He felt a sharp pain in his arm, and closed his eyes to escape it at least a little. When he opened them again he saw a large, strapping black man in front of him, clutching a Kalashnikov, and yelling, 'You little swine!'

He realized why his arm was hurting so much. A second, smaller and substantially stockier man had just chopped it off with his macheté. He instinctively wanted to grab hold of it, or at least what was left of it, but he could not. They forced him to the ground with their knees and prodded a flaming piece of wood into his wound. He fainted from the pain, and when he came round, the larger man bared his rotting teeth: 'We're not murderers. We're just protecting our children.'

He curled up into a ball, holding on to the stump, so horribly did it hurt. He realized that the world is an awful place and he regretted having been born into it.

Again Tomáš saw the well-known triangle. Now he was standing in it as a young one-armed man holding a knife. Immediately in front of him there were three of his most trusted men. As the triangle expanded he did not recognize many people. He saw his army with thousands of men and felt proud of them.

He moved elsewhere. Everything was atremble. All around him things were falling and breaking, everything was shaking and he prayed for it to stop. It took him some time to realize that he was in the middle of an earthquake. When the ground stopped shaking he went out to have a look. His half-demolished temple was surrounded by fallen buildings. He was barefoot, and the rubble cut into the soles of his feet. He saw many wailing women and broken men who had lost their loved ones. He was terribly sorry. He went to the local leader and asked him to help to search for survivors and to clear up the debris in the town, but he just fobbed him off.

'I can't help you. All my men are deployed in the war against the old regime, but we'll manage to get everything done much better once we've won. You have to understand that's more important than burying the corpses among the ruins.'

He was sure there were many more survivors in the ruins, but he could not guess how to save them, so he ran to the first demolished house that he saw and began to dig. He found one survivor and one corpse. There were dozens of houses like that in the village. As time passed by he found fewer and fewer of those who had survived this strong earthquake. From that time on he grew bitter and no longer trusted anyone. The world became a dark place for him.

He found himself at the tip of a triangle and in front of him were his devotees. He must have had a broad base, but he could not see all that far ahead. There were people as far ahead as he could see – thousands of them, all of them just as embittered and distrustful as he was.

He found himself above the globe, looking down at millions of flashes all over the world. He carefully examined one of them. A light was flickering like an expiring bulb, as if it wanted to shine with all its strength, but something was preventing it. After failing like this for some time, some of the lights stopped pulsating so often. They flickered less and less, until eventually they failed completely and a blank space appeared in their place. When other lights in the neighbourhood started to go out, a black hole began to expand and devour everything around. Entire states and nations were shrouded in darkness, with just a few little lights glittering within them, as they tried with all their might to keep at least a small flame glowing, even though the darkness was getting deeper and deeper.

His attention was drawn to what was going on above North America and immediately shifted over there. He was in his study, and everything was quiet. It didn't look as if he now faced the greatest decision of his life. North Korea had attacked Seoul with nuclear weapons, and as the US President and chief ally of South Korea he now had to adopt a clear position. He knew that an attack might provoke a third world war. He was also well aware that not to respond to such inhuman violence would be a sign of enormous weakness.

He thought of the millions of people all over the world. Some of them were praying, while others were waiting fraught at their television sets to see what America's answer would be to what had happened in Asia. Others were trying to get on with their lives, as if nothing had happened. He found himself there at this crucial moment! He breathed in deep and started to send the President and everybody else all the love and energy he had inside him. He knew very well that everything was at stake. He saw some of the flickering lights starting to pulse a little faster. One man was running for an important business meeting. He stopped for a moment, put twenty euros in a homeless man's frozen hand, looked him in the eye and wished him a nice day. The bulb flickered a few times and then came back on. The lights around it started to blink more intensively and some of them also lit up.

This was still not enough. Tomáš now became everything. He encompassed everything and became limitless love.

He saw a woman sitting in an office, waiting for a man who had applied for work at her company. It was up to her whether or not he was recommended. The interview went very well. The man had the necessary qualifications and was sincerely interested in the work. Then at one point he paused and managed with difficulty to spit it out that he had just been released from prison. The woman knew very well that she could not accept a former convict. If her boss found out he might well dismiss her. He's no philanthropist and he has no sympathy for this kind of thing, she thought. She closed her eyes, felt a gentle tickling inside her and remembered the child that she was expecting. She looked at the man who was quietly sitting opposite her and said, 'OK I like you. I shall recommend you.'

The man began to thank her with all his heart. Tomáš focused on the reaction that the woman's decision had provoked. It was like fireworks. He receded from that place and again looked at the globe. Now he saw millions of flickering lights and many that had lit up completely. Indeed the world was waging a struggle with itself. The most important choices in history were being made. Occasionally the flickering light died out completely, but here and there one of them totally lit up. He felt it was all very much on the edge. How it all ended up depended very much on individuals. He immersed himself completely and was determined to stay until the lights gained the edge.

Again he moved down to the White House. He was the Military

Supreme Commander with the largest number of nuclear warheads in the world. He connected to the world and wanted to know its view, but it did not have a view. One part said one thing and the other part said another. The first thought of retaliation and the other chose the light. He closed his eyelids and his entire life passed before his eyes. Without his being fully aware, the Monday morning when they diagnosed cancer in his wife flashed through his mind. When he opened his eyes again he was firmly decided. Atrocities like that must never be allowed to happen again, whatever it takes! He rushed out of his office, where his generals were waiting for him.

'The USA will defend its allies. We shall show them that we are not afraid with a preemptive nuclear attack.'

Tomáš could not breathe, and felt a strong pressure on his chest, as if an elephant were sitting on it. He writhed in agony as he glimpsed the Earth for the last time out of the corner of his eye. The lights were going out en masse, as a dark circle appeared over south-east Asia. He knew very well what this was.

He woke up sweating, and still unable to breathe, he gasped for breath, until he had calmed down enough to be able to think. Eliška was not next to him, and he was afraid for her. He did not know if it had been a dream or reality. He began to breathe deeply and put his feet on the floor. It was cold. He looked around the room, put his three fingers together and then realized – it was not morning, but evening. He had gone to bed tired after work and Eliška had come home late. When he went to check on the baby, it struck him as strange that he had not woken her up with his own noisy awakening. When Eliška saw him later that evening, she immediately noticed that something was not right. 'Why are you so pale?'

— • —

The next day he took off for the mountains, though the weather was

by no means ideal. It was cold and it rained heavily, so the ascent was not at all easy. The cold raindrops jabbed his face and he felt the sting as the tips of his toes froze. When he got to the summit, the skies suddenly cleared, and a magnificent view of the landscape opened up. He could even tell where it was raining and where it was not. Two weeks had passed since the last team meeting. Perhaps it was not their task to stop Musílek's ascent. Perhaps they had been unable to prevent it, because they had come together sooner than they should have, and they simply were not prepared. He came down from the mountains and felt a little better for several days.

3/29 Bomb attacks

Tomáš was awoken by Věrka's cries, so he went to look in the living room, where they were coming from. Eliška was sitting by the television, holding the baby in her arms, but without even trying to calm her down, as she herself was crying.

'What's happened?' he asked.

Eliška was so tearful that she could hardly speak: 'Bombs have gone off in banks all over the world. One of them was in Prague in Wenceslas Square.'

Her legs gave way beneath her and she had to go and sit down. A reporter was providing a description in a live broadcast.

'There's confusion everywhere. All you can hear is shouting and wailing sirens. The firemen are trying to get as many people as possible out to safety from the partially collapsed building. Several deaths and dozens of serious injuries have been confirmed. Ambulances and helicopters are taking the injured to hospitals all over Prague. I have never seen anything as horrific in all my life. Dear God!' He could barely be heard above all the noise.

The pictures showed people bleeding and wrapped in blankets. Firemen were bringing out more injured people from the taped-off area. He could not believe it and gave his family a hug. He was very glad that all three of them were now safe together.

'The people who died in the bank also had families,' he said with tears welling up in his eyes. He wanted to wake up again, so sure was he that it was just another dream.

'So much pain! How could anybody do this?'

The latest figures on bomb attacks all over the world were announced on the news. First estimates spoke of hundreds of fatalities. When he heard this, his heart seemed to come to a stop. He was no longer anxious over what the world might become. He was horrified by what the world already had become. There were children among the dead. Despair, emptiness and anger ate deep into him. His light went out.

For a long time they watched as the number of dead and injured rose. Bombs exploded all over Europe, America, Japan, India, Brazil and Russia. Everybody was trying to find out who was responsible. It had come like a bolt out of the blue. The police in most countries had most other banks evacuated and closed as a precaution. The underground trains stopped running along with other life in the big cities. The longer he sat in front of the television set, the more he realized how cruel and unjust the world was. His dream evaporated and the bubble in which he lived had burst. Now he finally admitted what a huge lie he had previously been living in, and this was a very painful insight. It was only now that he realized the world was a dark place. He embraced Eliška and, without believing it himself, whispered, 'It's gonna be all right.'

Sitting in front of the television would not help now, so he took the baby in his arms and went to give her a bath. He watched the stream of water gushing from the tap and wondered if this was not just another dream. He was torn away from his musings by Eliška's voice. 'I'll help you.'

When he looked at her face, he realized that he was not dreaming, and that the world had changed in the blink of an eye. Now he was even afraid to pop out to the shops. He was afraid to leave Eliška and the baby. He asked himself: How can you wake from a nightmare when you are not asleep?

— • —

They got back to the television in time. The announcer had just introduced a live broadcast of Musílek's rapidly convened press conference. He was perfectly well groomed as always.

'I wish I could have spoken to you in more pleasant circumstances. I have not yet officially been appointed Prime Minister, and yet I already have to lead my country in this difficult hour. I assure you that we are doing everything we can to find the culprits behind this senseless bloodshed as quickly as possible. Justice must be restored. The criminals expect society to be lenient towards them, and they are literally laughing in our faces,' he thundered. 'What is good and what is bad? Society is so confused these days with various glib opinions that it does not know. Together we have to teach it. We have to stand up against all those who have no values. We have to restore law and order!' and he pounded his fist on the rostrum. 'Only that way can we stop attacks similar to those we saw today. We have to make sure that order and justice come to be the internal values of each and every one of us,' and he looked around the hall. 'It is only this way that we will halt the collapse of society that has already begun. You only have to look to the north of this country. People there have no trust in each other and fear to go out at night. You call this 21st century democracy?' and he raised his arms sideways. 'Decent people are afraid to go out onto the street at night? How faithful is a hungry dog? Hence I am introducing free food for all citizens who adhere to the law in this country with immediate effect.' A murmur of approval passed over the hall. 'The world is corrupt and needs to be cleaned up. The wheat needs to be separated from the chaff. We should not confuse excessive sympathy for justice. We must not be sentimental,' and he leaned on the rostrum. 'Our enemies are not sentimental. Do you think they would not stab you in the back at night when no one is watching? And you want to be sympathetic to these people? Is this what you wanted? Our society today full of crime and despair?' and he raised his voice higher. 'Did you imagine the world this way? Too long have we listened to various idealists and utopians talking about endless love. That only leads to chaos and anarchy. Justice leads to law and order,' and he raised his head. 'People who do not see the long arm of the law up above them will soon turn rogue and be capable of stealing and killing. We have to show everybody that you cannot hide from justice. Vigilance is the price of our security. The experienced criminologists have gone and criminality is rising, because the criminals have become more experienced. Special police units are being set up to watch over our security,' and now he was suddenly speaking extremely quickly, 'so murderers, rapists and thieves will have no chance against them. Nor these bombers!' and he slowed his pace again. 'I shall do everything to ensure that border controls are reintroduced as soon as possible. There are many dangers here, particularly Muslims,' and he looked at his audience, as if he were now looking for them. 'Of course, we shall remain in contact with the European Union, even though it would be highly desirable if its member states realized that they need us more than we need them, so we shall be dealing with them accordingly from now on. Why should we subsidize irresponsible member states? Why, when we don't have any ourselves?' and he raised a clenched fist. 'The Chamber of Deputies will also pass a law on internal security as soon as possible to ensure that prisoners do not riot and escape from prison. As a result we will no longer have to live through anything like what has happened to-day. From now on we shall no longer fear to walk the streets at night. I will not allow any disturbances!' he shouted. 'A new social law is to be passed, which will ensure that loafers and idlers do not have more than decent, hardworking people,' and he fell silent for a moment. 'People like you,' and he extended his open palms towards the public.

'We are also working on a new corruption law, so that we can draw up lists of corrupt politicians and the punishments they will receive.'

'I promise work,' he thundered. 'I promise progress,' he said even louder. 'I promise justice!' he yelled. 'And above all I promise results!' he added triumphantly. Loud applause resounded throughout the hall. The audience rose from their seats and made no attempt to hide their enthusiasm.

'So this is the way it begins?' Tomáš said, clasping his head.

'I'm so sorry I didn't believe you at first,' Eliška sighed. 'You were right. All this time I thought you were living in your own reality, but it was me who couldn't see reality, or rather who didn't want to see it. But then what is and what isn't reality?' she asked him, as if he could tell the difference. At least she now finally understood his uncertainty and disunity a little – the constant zigzagging between the two worlds that he experienced every day.

He looked at her sympathetically. 'Actually, darling, I don't know what's real any more.'

3/30 The final meeting

I t occurred to Tomáš that the team would certainly want to call a meeting. He went to have a quick look at his mobile phone, which had been turned off since the day before.

'Please come to No. 53 as soon as possible.'

He washed his face and shakily started to dress.

'I have to see the team. I'll explain later.'

'What are you going to do with them?' Eliška asked uneasily.

'I don't know. We might go over what's happened today. Don't worry about me. It'll be safe, I'll be back in a couple of hours. Better stay home with the baby. I love you.'

'I love you too,' she said, snuggling up to him.

It was as if nothing happened between this hug and Tomáš's knock on the door at No. 53, because the next thing that he recalled was Kristýna opening the door. 'We thought you weren't coming!'

The talk was already in full flow. Kristýna was saying, 'The only way is simply to carry on with life and keep yourself occupied with something. To have no time to think about it.'

Karla did not agree with this. 'But we can't just pretend that nothing's happened! That would show a huge lack of respect for the people who didn't survive.'

'Bad things happen,' said Kristýna. 'We have to go on. We must not waste another day.'

'That is precisely what the people who have done this actually want,' said Dimitri. 'For us to fall into despair and stop living our lives.'

'Well one way or another,' said Tomáš, 'life is not going to be the same as it used to be.'

Jirka, who was evidently absorbed by the entire matter, agreed with him. 'Unfortunately you are right. Do you know that they've started to use the expression 'black hour', because all the bomb attacks took place within sixty minutes? One of my friends died there today.'

Kristýna stroked his shoulder: 'I am sorry.'

'Marek, do we know who might be behind it yet?' asked Dimitri.

'There are several possibilities. From terrorists to radical Communists to conspiracy theories,' said Marek.

'What kind of conspiracy theories?' asked Jirka.

'That it was all hatched by people linked to the government to divert people's attention from the problems they face.'

'In any case it's going to have a huge mental effect on people. Some will fall victim to despair, others to the doctrines of various despots, others will begin to deny reality, or to protest, while perhaps some will remain within their heart.'

Kristýna grew sad. 'Even though remaining in my heart is particularly difficult for me now, as I feel that enormous pain.'

He knew very well what she had in mind, because he could feel it too.

Marek leant back in his armchair: 'All over the world things are now awfully gloomy. These attacks have released something that has been bubbling away in people for a long time. Even in countries that are usually untroubled, such as China and Russia, enormous anti-government demonstrations have broken out. In Europe too. There have been dozens of deaths now in Hungary and Romania.'

Tomáš was now very well aware that his dreams were beginning to come true: 'We should be thinking up ways to calm the situation down, so it doesn't grow into a far worse catastrophe.'

'I think we should focus on Musílek,' said Dimitri. 'He's taken advantage of these bomb attacks. He's getting more and more powerful, and people of a similar kind are joining him. They see his growing influence and realize this is a way to get into power.'

Karla agreed. 'Yes, I saw his speech on television. I've never seen him looking so resolute. The strength that bristles in him sent a shiver down my spine. I am sure it must have had an enormous effect on people.'

Marek could see beneath the surface of all this. 'Except they are not aware of what he is doing behind their backs. He comes across as a defender of the public, but have you read his Internal Security Bill?'

'What's it like?' Kristýna asked.

Marek was disgusted. 'We really are not going to be afraid to walk the streets at night, because it is often going to be forbidden. The bill covers not only internet censorship, but also what pages you visit and what you do online. This act will make public television nothing but Musílek's propaganda tool, and under the veil of security he basically wants to do away with its independence. The act will expand police powers at the expense of our liberties. There is also a reference to a vice squad. This act gives the notion of the police state a completely new dimension.'

'That is awful,' said Karla, 'even though I do understand that people are going to agree to all this after what's happened. From now on, everybody who is different is going to be considered dangerous.'

'Except this involves not only state security but Musílek's secure tenure of power. He's taking advantage of the opportunity and highlighting our security, while drawing up more laws that have nothing to do with security, just to consolidate his position,' Marek pointed out.

'Such as?' Kristýna asked.

'Such as the Act on the Efficiency of State Administration, which amongst other things links up the banks, the state and the army. Or the new Anti-corruption Act, under which lists of people involved in corruption will be drawn up, with very harsh penalties for them.'

Jirka ironically added, 'Let me guess – there won't be any independent body to make sure that Musílek doesn't put away inconvenient people like me, for example.'

Marek nodded. 'Exactly. Then we have a new Labour Code. Not working will be a punishable offence, which means they'll be able to imprison the handicapped, the homeless and people who have simply been unable to find work.'

Kristýna was devastated by this: 'Good God!'

But Marek had not finished. 'There's also the Family Protection Act. Possession of any pornographic recordings will be punishable, as will be obscene behaviour in public, although nowhere is this defined, so they could lock you up for kissing someone in a shop.'

'Is there anyone who knows about this who might inform the public?'

'Yes, but Musílek has lots of supporters who say that finally they have somebody to put things in order, but that the establishment wants to discredit him.' Tomáš recalled his neighbour. When they had recently been chatting about Musílek, he had confided, 'We need a strongman to put things in order round here. It doesn't bother me at all that he's going to put restrictions on some things.' At this moment Tomáš understood how Hitler got into power – it is not that difficult if people allow it to happen.

'I just don't understand why people can't put two and two together!' said Jirka. 'We can't close the borders and remain in the European Union. We can't just dictate conditions to other countries.'

'People only see and hear what they want to,' said Tomáš. 'They will hear out anybody who promises to get rid of their problems. Uncertainty and fear have robbed them of their common sense. When Musílek gives them food, certainty and a sense of security then they in turn give him their silent consent to everything he's going to do. And he's quite persuasive when he says he'll protect them.'

Karla stood up: 'So what are we going to do about it?'

'One thing is for sure,' said Jirka. 'We have to attack immediately, before he consolidates his position.'

'Attack?' Tomáš blurted out.

Jirka also stood up and began to pace round the room. 'After meeting up with Dimitri, we have already taken the necessary measures. We have mobilized the opposition and tomorrow we are arranging an enormous demonstration in the centre of Prague.'

'But that might cost somebody their life!' Tomáš exclaimed. 'Musílek has announced that he's not allowing any disturbances! Why haven't you told us?'

'He must not remain in power,' said Dimitri. 'We had to act quickly. Several human lives are a small price to pay for the freedom of everybody.'

Tomáš was totally livid: 'Who are you to decide the price of a human life?! Nobody is to die! And do these people know that they might lose their lives?! Nobody has probably bothered to tell them that, have they?'

'They know it's a risk, but their patience has run out,' said Jirka. 'And if they have to, they will defend themselves. Musílek could harm you or your children with impunity any time. Don't you see that?'

But Tomáš had moved on elsewhere. Above him a gigantic helix spiraled up into the heavens, while below him another gigantic spiral plummeted down into a bottomless abyss. He realized what it all meant. He calmed down a little and placed his hand on Jirka's shoulder.

'I can't stand him just as much as you can't, and I am sorry about your friend, but violence only leads to further violence, and evil begets evil. If we use violence, we're no better than they are.'

'Don't hide your cowardice behind your respect for life,' said Dimitri, which really enraged Tomáš. He failed to understand how they failed to understand. As for killing, there could be no compromise.

'No one is forcing you to come along with us,' said Jirka. ' But then you can't compel us not to either. People are free and you can't prevent them from doing what they want to do.'

Tomáš sadly lowered his gaze and recalled his last dream. If humanity decides to destroy itself then there is no way that can be changed.

Jirka was looking for other allies within the team: 'How about you, Marek? Are you in with us? In your own way you are quite irreplaceable.'

Marek scratched the stubble on his face: 'Like a true Czech I'm going to wait for it to blow over.'

Tomáš still did not agree. 'There must be another way!'

Eventually Kristýna became involved. 'We have to stick together. We're strongest when we're together. I suggest we meditate now.'

'You know I respect you enormously, Kristýna,' said Jirka, 'but meditating is not going to help us now. I will be very happy, though, if you join us.'

'I don't have to join anybody,' she answered. 'I am on everybody's side. Still, I'm not supporting this event in the square. As always I shall do the best I can, and I shall send energy to all of you.'

'I do really appreciate that, Kristýna' said Tomáš. He looked urgently at Dimitri and Jirka and then said, 'Please think it over.'

'If one side puts down its weapons, the other side will begin its attack anyway. If they manage to stop the violence in one part of the world, it will break out in another part anyway. We have to stop this even at the cost of violence.'

'You want to stop violence with violence?'

His question caught Dimitri unawares. 'I don't think we are going to agree here. This is probably the end of our joint efforts. Go home. Tom, you stay with your family. Same goes for you others. We will be doing the fighting for you.'

This reminded Tomáš of Musílek when he was trying to convince him that this was not his struggle.

'How about you, Karla?' Jirka asked.

'I'm not going to stand by and watch.'

There was nothing else for it, but to go for his coat, and Tomáš started putting it on. Kristýna came up behind him, but before she managed to say anything he asked her, 'Are we going to carry on even if no hope is left? To fight on even if there is no point? Why?!'

As always she looked tenderly at him. He noticed what a marvellously beautiful face she had.

'Why do we fall? So that we can stand up again.'

'But I don't think we're going to stand up again after this fall. It's a deep abyss.'

She stroked his face. 'The tree is often destroyed by the storm or the strong wind. Only part of the trunk remains. And yet new life will grow from it in the springtime. We do not see what is down there beneath the soil where the tree has its roots. Do you remember how we talked about putting together those jigsaw pictures? We never know how they'll turn out.'

'I only see darkness.'

Kristýna embraced him. 'It is darkest before the dawn.'

These words went through him like arrows, warming his tense, cold body. He walked down the stairs and went outside. Heavy, almost black clouds were floating over the city. It would soon rain.

'So the end begins this way?'

He felt solitude seeping through. He had almost forgotten what it was like to feel absolute futility. His soul made itself heard: *I am always with you. You will never be alone.*

He was glad to be able to go back home to Věrka and Eliška. He did not know how long it would last, but he lived here and now, and preferred not to think about the future much. Now he wanted to be with them.

Again and again he thought over everything, unable to release it from his mind. Darkness loomed over the world, and he could do nothing about it. The first drops of rain began to fall on the dirty pavement. No matter how hard he tried, the equation had no other solution. It was clear to him that because of the violent protests on the square, another wave of repression would be coming.

The road to hell is paved with good intentions, he thought.

People's behaviour clearly spoke of a future that he had seen in his dreams. Perhaps we won't get another chance. Perhaps we don't deserve another one, he thought. Our children will have to pick up the pieces that we have left them and build a better world out of them. He was sorry that Věrka would grow up in a place like this. When he arrived home, wet through, Eliška embraced him.

'My folk are here.'

'I'm glad to see you,' and he hugged her.

'Musílek wants to leave the European Union and other countries are probably going to follow suit. He also wants to double the number of police and to censor the internet. I am sorry I didn't believe you at first.'

'Fighting for a better world is important, but not at the expense of you and Věrka. I'm sorry I didn't understand that previously, but now I shall stay home.'

They kissed and went into the living room to see her parents, who were playing with the baby. Tomáš was never very keen on these family gatherings, but this time he felt completely different about it. He was glad he could be with his nearest and dearest. His sister was there too. He and Eliška sat next to her and watched the grandparents playing around with the baby, who was in her element and kept laughing. Outside it was raining heavily. The raindrops drummed on the roof. Tomáš felt happy and safe for at least a little while. He remembered Kohl once telling him: 'Stay connected. The bad feelings won't go away, but you'll be able to deal with them a lot better.'

'If Kohl were here now and saw what was going on, what might he say?'

When he went to bed he knew he would have his nightmares again, but he no longer cared. For a long time he had been afraid of his dreams, but now he had a far greater dread, as the world turned into what he had seen in them. There was nothing to be done about them. He had the feeling he did not belong to this world full of evil and pretence. He had changed so much over the last few years, he was now a considerably better person than he had been. Ever since he met Kohl, he had constantly tried to change the world for the better. He had overcome various obstacles and got over times of despair and always got up again. And yet it had all been to no avail. People really do not want to live in a world without suffering. If they wanted to, they would have chosen to do so a long time ago. It was quite irrefutable. Why had he been wasting so much effort all this time?

— • —

When Kristýna arrived home, her little boy Adam was waiting for her. 'Mummy, mummy! I'm so glad you're home,' and he leapt into her arms. As they ate supper together a storm raged outside. The rain drummed against the windows as a gale blew outside. Soon afterwards the electricity went down.

'Not to worry. At least we'll have some peace and quiet for meditation,' Kristýna smiled at him.

'I'm already looking forward to that. Who are we going to save today?'

'If we succeed, then the whole world, Adam,' and she stroked his dark, curly hair.

He jumped around for joy, shouting 'Yippeee.'

She lit several candles. They sat opposite one other and held each other's hands. Then she said: 'Remember how you felt last time. Your mind floated above the world and you admired how beautiful it was. Do you see it?'

Joyfully he nodded, and she asked: 'How do you feel?'

'Like a penguin and a daisy and a hedgehog and a raindrop and the sun and dance...' It made nice listening. Adam was still going on as she fell into a deep state of meditation.

She smelled the fragrance of strong green tea. The air was heavy due to the approaching storm. She looked into her brother Ho-Kin's eyes. They had just been talking about how the Chinese government was weak and might soon fall. This made her brother terribly worried. There was a clap of thunder, which here in the mountains always awakened in her a sense of holy respect for nature.

When she again opened her eyes, she saw a tall, craggy mountain range. She was carrying a knapsack, and his wife was telling her about the high tensions in the region. She knew that women should not talk about politics much, but she always felt free to do so in their family, and they often discussed politics together. Xia Ji was worried by the Iranian nuclear programme, increasing poverty in Palestine and the political unrest in Israel. She was afraid the conflict would escalate into war. For a while she stopped, looked into the cloudless sky and wiped her perspiring forehead. It was hot.

When she looked around again she was in Brno, discussing the Musílek situation with her friend the priest. Jakub had addressed her with his doubts: 'If God has his plan then only He understands it.'

'It's easy to have faith and enthusiasm when everything is going smoothly, but true faith means deciding to believe even in the darkest moments,' she answered him.

She breathed in deep and found herself back home. Her youngster's eyes were still closed. She realized that she had seen three epicentres. Unless someone stepped in soon then something awful was going to happen there, which would grow into a worldwide conflict. She rather regretted the fact that she had recently been attempting to deal with the Musílek issue and had neglected the dangers looming elsewhere. She waited for Adam to come round, and then she put him to bed. She decided to meditate all night. She would raise her own energy level and subsequently those of all the inhabitants in those regions. She would appeal to all people of good will to add their love to the system.

3/31 Escape from the shelter

Tomáš woke up in a hospital bed with a dry throat. He could barely swallow. Hoarse and wheezy, he asked an elderly nurse for some water. The water tasted as if he had licked a toilet bowl. As soon as he had had a drink he managed to get talking.

'Wh-what happened?'

'You were attacked by some zeros. Normally they kill their victims straight away, but they only kicked you unconscious. I'd say you only survived thanks to a miracle, if I still believed in miracles. I'm only sorry you haven't been put out of your misery.'

'Zeros? What zeros? Last thing I remember, I was shopping with my wife!'

The gaunt woman with broad shoulders took off her glasses. 'That blow to your head has probably made you lose your memory. You've got a fine bruise here on your side.' She touched the spot and he gave a howl. 'Do you really want to hear? In your shoes I wouldn't.'

He drank up what was left of the water, leaving just an imperceptible pool at the bottom of the metal mug, and nodded.

As the nurse began to talk, he noticed she had several teeth missing. 'It began with minor attacks. Drinking water was poisoned in a couple of places, and from time to time a bomb exploded in a supermarket. The government kept saying that foreign terrorist groups were responsible. We believed them. Then came the first black-out. Fortunately it only lasted three days.'

He looked around and tried to figure out where he was. He did not recognize anything here. It looked more like a garage than a hospital here – a really bleak-looking garage.

The nurse was staring at her wrinkled palms as she mumbled on. 'At first the internet was down sporadically, for a couple of hours or so, but eventually it went down completely, along with the shops, banks and state administration. This caused enormous chaos, and the government kept looking for culprits. Then there were more black-outs, and the world as you know it ceased to exist.'

She stopped talking for a while and just breathed out loud. 'People stopped trusting one other and society fell apart. Hunger and disease became widespread – children stopped smiling. Suicides were just as frequent as births. Then came the first nuclear attack. In the ensuing chaos everybody wanted to get inside the shelter, but unfortunately there was only space in them for the chosen few. And before we got inside, the government finally worked out who was responsible for it all. All that time we had been expecting an external enemy. We were afraid the Chinese, Russians or Arabs were attacking us. We were so absorbed with what was going on outside that we had totally underestimated what might be coming from within. It was terrorists from Europe who were responsible for most of the attacks. They called themselves the "New World".'

One by one his memories started coming back to him. He remembered getting into the shelter. Several people had been trampled to death in the stampede. He remembered three robbers attacking him in the dark tunnel. They were about twelve years old and they kicked him until he lost consciousness. He tried to get up out of bed, but the nurse stopped him. 'Better leave that till tomorrow. You have nowhere to go in a hurry. Nobody hurries much here any more.'

He was going to ask about his wife, but he remembered she had died long before. He started trembling with the cold. The nurse covered him up and left without saying anything.

— • —

When they released him the next morning he went to see Pavel. He had seriously considered suicide before he met him. I'd never have believed just how much one person can influence your life, he thought. Pavel was not in the dormitories, so Tomáš went to have a look in the common room, but he didn't find him there either. He asked a couple of people if they had seen him, but they all made out they hadn't. There was nothing else for it but to go to the police. He was afraid, because the local 'lawmen' were extremely harsh and uncompromising. The very fact that he went there of his own accord could cause him huge problems.

The police officer looked at him contemptuously and mumbled something to the effect that he had to check in the records, abruptly adding, 'Sit down here and don't move.'

The longer Tomáš waited, the more nervous he became. After a while the bald police officer with protruding ears came back:

'That man was executed. Somebody saw him giving the zeros some food. Why are you actually here? Where do you know him from?'

He knew that if he admitted to being his friend then they would probably kill him too. 'The swine robbed me. I thought I'd find him and get my things back.'

The police officer had the expression of an enraged pitbull. 'If I'd known you came here over some bollocks like that I wouldn't have bothered to find out. Now clear off!'

He left and went round the corner, where he leant against a wall resignedly. The cold and damp from the mouldy walls gradually seeped into his body. If it hadn't brought about huge problems he would not even have gone in to teach today, but it was one of the reasons why he received such privileges as five minutes of showering a week and food every day. When he got to the classroom there were again fewer children sitting there. Their numbers kept falling, as they died from various diseases. After the class he was approached by one girl, whom he remembered from the past. Her pink dress was dirty, her face was bruised and it did not escape him that her arms had been pierced. It was a harrowing sight: such a small girl and her veins were as damaged as those on the forearm of a veteran drug addict. Tomáš felt some emotion for the first time in a long time. He asked her her name.

'They call me Věrka.' Her right eye was bloodshot as she looked at him.

'That's a very nice name. What happened to you, Věrka?' and he pointed to her bruised arms.

'I don't want to eat, so they try to keep me alive this way,' and she acted as if she were answering some routine question.

'Why don't you want to eat, Věrka?'

'Because I want to get out and nobody's listening to me. I shall keep sulking like this, until they let me out.' She wrinkled her brow.

'But you can't get out. Nobody can get out. We wouldn't survive out there, because of the radiation.'

'That's rubbish!' she exclaimed. 'Will you take me out there please?'

'That isn't possible,' and he wrapped up his things and set off to the dormitory. As he walked through the dark tunnel a light flickered here and there, revealing his sorry state. A thought occurred to him: What if it's all one big lie? What if it's all just propaganda to keep us underground? Perhaps that's why they got rid of Pavel. I shall have to find out!

He dropped his books and ran back into the school. The girl would definitely be in the recreation room. He ran to it and found her playing with the other children. He called out her name, but she did not respond. He walked right up to her and whispered, 'Shall we get out together then now? You have to be quiet and go through the door behind me, right?'

Now she was nodding in excitement, and he quietly walked out. The supervising teacher did not even notice. When she left, he took her by the hand and they set out together. He knew that if they caught him they would kill him. Kidnapping a child or harming it in any way was the worst crime possible in those difficult times, because they were needed to maintain the human population. He had found out from Pavel that there had been landslides and cave-ins in the tunnels to the south. He had said this might have opened a way out. He chose that route to avoid all the security patrols, quite successfully as it turned out.

The girl's feet were now aching, so he carried her for a while. It was quiet all around and they saw no one alive. Law and order were not supervised in these remote corners of the shelter, so now and then they would see a corpse lying on the ground. Hence the ever-present stench – a kind of strangely sweetish smell. This did not upset his small companion at all. She just sometimes held her nose when the stench became too intense.

He noticed some shadows in the distance and went totally stiff. After a while he heard indistinct voices. He picked her up and they hid behind a heap of debris just a little way off. A police patrol came up through the tunnel. If they found him here with a child they would shoot him on the spot.

The police approached, lighting up the tunnel walls with their torches more and more. He covered her mouth. 'It's now very, very important to be totally quiet, do you understand? Otherwise we won't get out.' She nodded. As they passed by, the splashing that accompanied them suddenly stopped. They stood on the spot and looked around, as their torchlight shone directly at the heap of debris. Splash splash! One police officer was right next to them. He was so close that they could see the time on his gold wristwatch, and they could hear him breathing. Tomáš's limbs went numb with fear and he could not move. The police officer seemed to bend down for something, a jolt shuddered through the tunnel and a corpse fell into the water just a little way off.

'You'll like that,' he headed back to his colleague, and Tomáš felt an enormous sense of relief.

After a couple of minutes of silence he calmed down a little and again found himself able to move, so they set out. The little girl complained, 'I'm hungry.'

'Not to worry. We'll be there soon.'

He realized that even if they made it to the surface, he had no way to look after her, but it was too late to think of going back now. They were definitely being looked for.

Something like daylight could now be seen at the end of the tunnel. He took her in his arms and began to run in that direction. Behind them they heard, 'Stop or you're dead!'

He did not obey but ran on. He heard splashing water behind them, and guessed there were at least two police officers, but he did not have the courage to turn round. After a while he reached the place where the light came from. It was not daylight but came from a manhole in the ceiling with a ladder leading to it. He raised the girl as high as he could:

'Quick, get up there!'

He gasped with difficulty and climbed up behind her. Suddenly he felt a sharp pain and immediately realized that they were shooting at him and had hit him in the chest. He began to close the heavy steel lid behind him as the police officer's hands reached out for them. He trod on the man's fingers. He fell back in and Tomáš closed the lid. It took him a while to get used to the clear light. The corridor was full of food and other supplies.

'This must be where they store the goods that come from outside. There might be more police around,' he said out loud. He looked around the corridor and tried to find something like an exit. He found another hatch. Nothing hurt now, but he was almost out of breath and he was coughing blood. The bullet had probably hit his right lung. He took some food from an open crate, helped the little girl up and out and then closed the lid behind him.

Now they found themselves in another corridor, at the end of which they could clearly see daylight. It was so wonderful. At the other end it was black as pitch.

They set off for the light, and the girl began to grin. 'I told you so! I told you so!' The glow became brighter and brighter. After a couple of minutes he could hardly walk. They were almost there, when they heard shouts from the dark end of the tunnel. The girl began to cry, and with his last strength he took her by the hand and started running, but he tottered and fell, with foul-tasting water in his mouth. He wanted to stay lying there, but she helped him up.

'Nearly there, nearly there. You'll make it. You must! '

He took several rapid steps and felt a sharp pain in his spine. Another bullet. He fell down and felt his life escaping from him. He closed his eyes.

When he opened them again he saw a tree. It was a healthy, sturdy oak. He was still lying on the ground, but nothing was hurting now and he could breathe normally. Věrka sat below him, looking completely different now. He barely recognized her. She was barefoot and left neat footprints in the grass around her. She wore a lovely, ironed, pink dress. Her face was a healthy colour with marvellous combed hair with which the wind played and through which the sun shone. She was so clean and innocent. Tomáš breathed in deep. The air was full of the fragrance of grass.

Věrka was drawing on paper with coloured pencils. Her model was a little puppy lying in front of her and playing with a blue ball. It was so wonderful and colourful. He slowly stood up and walked down towards them. He felt marvellous! He had no shoes on, so he immediately felt the blades of grass beneath his feet. He remembered the cold, wet, rough floor of the shelter. He could smell the cold, damp, grimy concrete. He had thought that he would never again experience a feeling like walking on fragrant grass. Or like looking at the daylight. Now the shelter and the memories on it were indescribably far away.

He was now filled with an endless joy and peace. The grass pleasantly cooled and tickled his feet. When the puppy saw him it began to bark merrily and leap around. Věrka was beside herself with joy.

'Hello Daddy! Hello Daddy!' Her hands were as soft as the hands of a new-born baby and the bruises had disappeared. Her dress smelled of lavender. Tomáš felt the warmth and love as they embraced. The feeling enveloped him entirely, and lasted an eternity. Suddenly everything became clear and he no longer felt any conflict. All the tension had gone. He was in heaven and would remain there forever. His soul rejoiced and happily sang. He felt so glad that something so marvellous had come from him – something as pure as Věrka. She smiled at him and said, 'It isn't too late yet.'

When he awoke he was still in a state of indescribable bliss. And he knew what he had to do.

3/32 The square

Eliška's hair cooled him pleasantly. He got up quietly so as not to awaken her. He felt his heart beating. He quickly put a couple of things in his rucksack. He looked at Eliška and remembered seeing her for the first time. That night neither they nor their friends went to bed, but danced till dawn. She wore a beautiful dress and was full of life, completely spellbinding him. In the morning they exchanged numbers and agreed to meet again somewhere they could hear each other and have a chat.

He entered the baby's room as quietly as possible. He had to see Věrka. She lay on her side in her cot with a little finger in her mouth. He was now fully aware of what he was about to do. It was the most difficult decision in his life. All it needed was for the baby to open her eyes and he would no longer have been able to go. But she slept on peacefully. She had no idea what was going on in the world. She had no idea what humanity was hurtling towards. She had no idea that her father wanted to do something as desperate as this.

One last look and an affectionate caress. When he saw the birthmark on her left cheek, tears welled up in his eyes, and he thought, I will do anything for you.

He glanced at her one last time and quietly closed the door to the room. He had taken a decision that was more difficult than most people on the planet were ever able to make. He felt it was totally correct. His reason did not understand, but his soul did. And humbly he followed it.

When he left the building it was still dark outside. It was cold and the streets were empty. He got in his car and started up the engine. After a moment of thought he set off. There was now dense mist

He recalled the time he had been talking to Kohl about total awakening. He asked himself: Is this where I am heading? Will I understand why this is happening?

On the motorway the number of cars increased as he approached Prague. He was beset by doubts. Even if he managed to succeed today, this would have no influence on the conflicts elsewhere in the world. He was so small and the world was so vast. Still, he listened to the voice of his soul and kept driving. Even though he did not know what he was to do or if it would help in any way at all, he felt joy and humility.

Eliška's face came to mind. It was so wonderful and soft. Then he envisioned Věrka's face. They were so similar. It was daylight when he switched off the engine and got out. He could go no further in the car. Driving into the centre was banned due to the disturbances. He left it parked on the bridge a little way from the main station. He then set off for the Old Town Square. With every step he thought less and less and felt his soul more and more. The number of people in the streets was increasing. Had they come to see what was going on, or did they want to take part?

He had to elbow his way through the last few metres to the square. As soon as he saw the police barriers he stopped. How am I going to get in? he wondered. He asked one bystander why the square was closed off.

Surprise in his face, the foreigner backed away. 'Lots of people have met up there to protest against some dictator. The police have closed it off so nobody else can join them. They want to get the situation under control.'

Tomáš stood in the middle of the crowd and observed. It was a strange feeling. His eyes fixed on two police officers. The younger one struck him as odd. He was a strapping young man. Tomáš walked up to him and looked him straight in the eyes.

'I'm here on Mr Musílek's personal order. I'm to get among the demonstrators and work in secret.'

The police officer looked at him distrustfully, but Tomáš did not avoid his gaze.

'Well, I don't have any instructions like that.'

'It's not official if you get my drift. Go ahead and call your commanding officer. He'll verify it with Musílek,' and he kept him fixed with his gaze. The police officer avoided his eyes. For a moment he looked a little frightened, as if he was perhaps afraid he might get into trouble over it.

'Go on then.'

As soon as he entered the square he faced a breathtaking scene. The people there were divided into two camps. On the right hand side of the square the police units were lined up tight, defending Musílek. All his other supporters had stayed at home in the knowledge that the police would take care of the regime's opponents. There were several thousand of them in the square. They had gathered on the left-hand side. That crowd was not organized at all. The police had put up a fixed barrier in front of their lines. They were armed and totally determined to defend national stability.

Opposite stood the demonstrators, who were angry and emotional. They did not intend to accept a return to the Middle Ages. They wanted to fight the dictator. They wanted to show their unity in the face of someone who failed to respect basic civic rights. Tomáš slowly looked over the motley crowd and was horrified to find young children among them. He was frightened to death and yet at the same time totally calm. He fully perceived all those emotions. The square was full of them. It was so easy to get carried away by them.

He felt the tension in every cell of his body, although deep within him he also felt heavenly peace. His soul spoke to him: *The world will fall apart if the people stop perceiving the beauty within it.* He realized that he was not standing on either side, but on both. He understood the sense of security that the strong leader gave to the frightened people. And he understood the sense of grievance shared by his opponents.

His soul spoke again: *You don't have to do this!*

But he was doing this, for the simple reason that it struck him as being right and that he himself wanted to do it. Most other people were there out of some kind of compulsion. He thought: If we are just looking for evil then the world is evil. If people only listen to their reason then the world becomes a dark place.

He cast aside the last of his doubts and took the first step. He gave up his all to heaven on high and stepped forward. He felt his feet touching the paved surface of the square. The world had slowed down. He saw the dark outline of the sun hidden behind the thick clouds. At a slow pace he approached the space between the two crowds. One of his voices was saying, Run, run! Don't turn round, just run! The other tried to put him off. Stand still! It's too big for you. You're just an ordinary person. Leave this to others.

Do you feel your heart in your chest? Do you feel it beating? Tomáš's soul asked.

Yes, it makes us who we are. He kept walking step by step and was more and more in his heart, which grew a little with every step. He was aware of each leg rising and falling.

Slowly he got to the space between the two sides, no man's land. The police in the front lines began to aim their pistols. People in the crowd to his left began to shout. Each side thought he was just a stooge put there by the opponents. The people and the police in the back rows noticed something was going on. He held his hands out high with unclenched fists. He felt the gazes of thousands of eyes. His awareness was expanded and he could clearly hear what several people were saying to him all at once. He could also feel why they were saying it. He felt the emotions of thousands of bodies. He could feel the fear. It seeped through him like frost. He could also feel the enormous love that radiated from within. He felt a wave of love surging over the entire square, but hidden beneath tons of fear. No one else on the square saw this. Only he did.

All those to the left were so angry, but love radiated from each of them. The police on the right tried not to show their emotions, but he could look into their hearts and feel what they were feeling. He felt Musílek's presence. For the first time it was no longer unpleasant, and Tomáš no longer feared him. Everything fit into place. He understood why things were happening that way. He understood that the truth belonged to everyone. And at last he could accept that Kohl had died.

With each step his legs grew heavier and his breathing became more laboured. He got to the point between the lines and sat down on the cold paving. He did not say anything and barely moved, although he had become the centre of attention. All the anger of the people in the square was now focused in his direction. Suddenly he was the one who was to blame for it all. All those thoughts and feelings. There were so many of them! It all now boiled down to a single thought and a single feeling: *You are the light, so shine! Become something greater!*

He then felt the tension and stress in all those people starting to recrystallize as something else. He could perceive their souls slowly connecting. All over the square the lights began to flicker, and some of them came on. He was no longer the only one. The world had come to a halt.

The police received an order. Get rid of that madman!

They spoke to him and warned him to leave immediately, but he did not move. The police in the front rows began to feel nervous. They did not know what to do with him. He was sitting there quietly, unarmed and prepared for anything, which aroused in them an incredible sense of admiration and humility. Here they stood armed and protected against somebody who was totally unarmed and peaceful, when they received the order to shoot him. Someone like that was too dangerous for Musílek.

The officer who received the order put down his gun, saying, 'I can't.' His colleague received the same instruction. Even though he knew he was ending his career in the force, he put down his weapon too. A third officer who received the order to shoot also pointed his gun to the ground. 'Sod it! I'm not getting saddled with that!' The others did not wait for the order and began to point their guns to the ground. It was an astonishing sight. The people in the square, many with mouths agape, watched as one police officer after another pointed his weapon to the ground.

All of them started to understand what was going on, and all their fears, misunderstandings and hatred started to disappear. The darkness that had enshrouded the square until now slowly began to evaporate.

But one youngster standing about twenty metres from Tomáš could not understand what was going on. None of this fit in with his worldview. He could not imagine a world without wars and killing. He pulled out his gun, aimed and squeezed the trigger.

The shot rang out all over the square, and the people around crouched down. They were most surprised that the shot had not come from the police but from the demonstrators themselves. Tomáš was suddenly knocked down to the ground by the bullet. It came so unexpectedly. His body fell to the ground like a rag doll. Police officers promptly disarmed the attacker. The people made way for them. The police approached the man with guns raised and he instantly surrendered.

A woman ran out shouting from among the demonstrators. After a while Tomáš realized it was Karla:

'Christ! Have you all gone mad? Call a doctor!'

The police officers in the front row raised their guns and aimed at Karla, who was running towards them. They watched to see what would happen. She knelt down beside him and looked over his wound.

'Good God, Tom. What have we done to you? Forgive us.'

When they realized she was not a threat they stopped aiming at her. People quietly watched what was happening in the middle of the square. The crowd opened up a space for a doctor, and a medical team came running through towards Tomáš, while an ambulance wailed behind them. Both sides came together and gathered around him and Karla. A cameraman appeared next to them from somewhere. Karla pressed his wound and quietly said:

'Please breathe. Eliška and Věrka are waiting for you at home.' With her other hand she stroked his face. Her face was tear-sodden.

Tomáš was very glad she was with him. He looked at her and smiled. She stroked him again. There was an awful whistling in his left ear. He felt no pain, just a chill, as his body was lying on the cold ground. His shoulders were warm from the blood beneath his body. His heart was beating faster and faster. He did not feel wronged at what had happened to him. He felt no anger towards the gunman. He only felt endless sadness that he would never again cradle Věrka, make love with Eliška or climb another mountain. The ground became warmer and warmer as his body grew cold. Somebody moved him, and he heard voices above him, but he could not make them out. They were so far away now. He felt the total emptiness. He could not guess what would come next. There was nothing else to seize onto except nothingness. For the first time in his life he was not afraid to embrace the darkness, as it lit up. The cold dissipated. Only the light remained.

3/33 A new beginning

When Adam awoke, his mother was still sleeping beside him. He stretched dozily and ran off to the living room to turn on the television. He was interested to see if his evening with mum had saved the world. The announcer was reading out the main news.

'China has seen the biggest anti-government protests for the last fifty years. The government was aiming to violently suppress them, but something has happened that would have been unthinkable even yesterday. The Communist Party has agreed with the opposition on key changes in the system. The main cause behind these bloodshed-free changes was the heroic act of a sixteen-year-old girl, who sat in the path of a tank. There has been unofficial talk of granting Tibet independence from China after fifty years.'

'More trailblazing news,' she smiled. 'Iran has said goodbye to its nuclear research. The leading scientists who have been behind the programme over the last few years have decided to end it, as one of their colleagues died in an attempt to disarm several nuclear warheads. The Iranian government has decided not to proceed with the programme. However, the most interesting news comes from home. Jan Musílek, the former Police Commissioner and leader of the Labour and Justice Party, will not become Prime Minister. After events at the Old Town Square, police units renounced allegiance and the army refused to intervene against citizens of the Czech Republic, so we are soon expecting early elections.'

The announcer then welcomed some wise-looking chap in a white sweater to the studio, who said, 'Thousands of people could have died. Perhaps tens of thousands, but these three stood up against it. They staked their own lives for the good of us all, but alas not all of them survived. Is one human life more valuable than thousands of others? Even if it is a person who does not hesitate to lose it for the good of others? It was not some organized movement. Each of them was acting on their own initiative and did not guess that at the other end of the world other people were also literally placing themselves in the front line, just like they were. None of them used violence and yet they managed, I daresay, to change the course of human history.'

'What kind of changes do you think this will bring about worldwide?'

'Within a short space of time ordinary people have managed to achieve things that politicians worldwide have been trying to achieve for many years. There is a clear message for us here. In Europe most people did not go into work today. Tomáš's pupils agreed overnight and took today off, but they did not stay at home. They have put on white garments and gone out into the streets carrying improvized white flags made of sheets and curtain rails. They are meeting up in the streets and just chatting – some with their relatives, others with their friends and still others with people they have never seen in their lives.'

All these people believe that Tomáš would have liked this. Some are a little perplexed by them. The faces of some lit up with a smile out of genuine interest, while others were moved to tears. The fear that stung us to the core and tormented us over the past months has disappeared. I am filled with new hope. As long as there are people like Tomáš we are going to live in a beautiful world. We now face some difficult tasks. We have to create a new political and economic system, but we now have the most difficult part behind us. We have overcome despair.

There are millions of Tomáš's pupils and they have flooded the streets of most European cities. We are now beginning anew and this has been a promising start. We can create a new world – the kind that we want. A world that we will be proud of. Thousands of people also gathered in front of the hospital where yesterday they fought for Tomáš's life. He has become a hero for us all – a model and a spiritual teacher. He reminded us of the best within ourselves. He showed us that it is better to die for a loving world than to live in a world without love and understanding. I keep thinking of a phrase he came out with during that interview: 'I don't want to live in a world where people have forgotten what they are."

The announcer, wearing a white blouse, smiled: 'Thank you, Václav. I'm glad you reminded us of that interview. It's just incredible how the recording managed to escape Musílek's men and the destruction they caused. One young colleague of ours was so inspired by him that she took a copy of her recording home. Over the last few hours, the video has been viewed online by over two hundred million users. Now let's go and have another look...'

'Aren't you afraid? Obviously, you are risking your life by sitting here today and speaking to the camera.'

He answered as he felt fit: 'I am afraid, but that doesn't stop me from doing something that I believe is the right thing to do.'

'How did you get to know these people?'

He described what had happened since he had got to know Naďa. He knew that some people would not believe this, but he did not care. He was happy to speak as he felt fit. His narrative ended with the abduction.

'What impression did Mr Musílek make on you during this interrogation?'

'First he tried to intimidate me and then after a while he started acting like my best friend. He said it wasn't my fight and that I should leave it all to him. That is precisely what is so dangerous about him. It is very easy to fall for his charisma and his spurious concern, but all he is really interested in is his own personal advantage. Anyone who has a different view to his has to get out of his way. One way or another. I'm not surprised at the people who let themselves be taken in by him. I believed him myself for a while, so I'm not guilt-free myself. I believed him that it's not my fight.'

'And is it your fight?'

'It is everybody's fight. If we fight for a better world, we show each other that we are human. If we fight for what we believe is right then we are actually alive.'

'Why are you doing this? Why are you taking such a risk? Aren't you afraid for the safety of your family and yourselves?'

'It is precisely because I have somebody important in my life that I am sitting here with you. It's only a pity that my wife and daughter aren't here with me. I would very much like you to get to know them. Even an idiot like me has had the good fortune to have such a marvellous family. I want my daughter to grow up in a free and just world. I want Věrka to grow up in a world where instead of telling her what to think and how to feel, others are interested in what she feels. A world without intimidation and one-sided solutions. A world where happiness is the meaning of life. If you are only interested in results, but not in how they are achieved then that is bad. We have to take some risks and make sure that people like Musílek do not get into power in this country.'

'Isn't that all a little naive?' asked Iveta.

'It is naive to think that we can carry on the same lifestyle as we have previously. It is naive to think that humanity can survive the problems that we face without love, understanding and caring for one another. It is also naive to think that we can use violence on others, without ourselves being harmed.'

'What kind of problems do you have in mind?'

'I have dreams that have been recurring for some time now. In all of these dreams people are struggling for their bare existence. They burrow down into underground shelters, and such things as hope, faith, trust and love have disappeared. I don't want to live in a world where people have forgotten what they are.'

'And do you think that all this will really happen?'

'If people listen to their hearts, forgive themselves after each lapse, dust themselves down and carry on where their souls are taking them, then this will certainly not happen. If we fight then we have nothing to fear. If we use our hearts as weapons then we become something greater. We will make this world much more than it is now. Much more than we can imagine in our most wonderful imaginings. We can create a heaven on earth. I am here to remind people of this, just as a friend of mine used to remind me.'

'Thank you, Tomáš.'

Published by Jakub Trpiš, Czech Republic
info@jakubtrpis.com
www.jakubtrpis.com

Original version published 2012
English translation published 2018 (1st edition)

Translated by Melvyn Clarke
Cover illustration by Martina Světlíková
Graphic design by Magda Kadlecová
Printing and binding by FINIDR, s.r.o., Czech Republic

ISBN: 978-80-907044-4-2